Going Global

A look at Daniel and his ministry

About the Author

Terry Young's parents were missionaries in the Middle East who settled the family in the Midlands in the early '70s. He was educated at the local grammar school, the local sixth form college and then the local redbrick. After 17 years in Essex, working in industry, he and Danielle moved to Berkshire and a new post in academia. His research interests lie in communication and information systems, and have focused on healthcare for the past eight years. Terry and Danielle have a family of three sons and worship at the local Baptist church.

Going Global

A look at Daniel and his ministry

Terry Young

Published by

and

First published 2008 by Partnership and Paternoster

14 13 12 11 10 09 08   7 6 5 4 3 2 1

British Library Cataloguing in Publication Data
A catalogue record for this book is available from the British Library.

ISBN 978-0-900128-36-3

Typeset by Toucan Design, 25 SouthernhayEast, Exeter.

Produced by Jeremy Muditt Publishing Services, Carlisle,
and published by Partnership and Paternoster Press,
PO Box 300, Carlisle, Cumbria CA3 0QS.

Printed and bound in Great Britain
by Bell and Bain Ltd, Glasgow.

To my mother, Joann and the memory of my father, Harry

Contents

Preface

On the edge

It was chemistry practical with maybe a dozen sixth formers, and the atmosphere was relaxed. We got on pretty well as a group and chattered light-heartedly across the benches while we got on with our titration, synthesis, or whatever it was. That afternoon everyone seemed to have some reason why life as a student was a bit of a pain. There was a chap in the corner whose motorbike and snooker cue were competing vigorously with his academic career. Tut-tutting mournfully, he told us that we shouldn't moan – after all, our schooldays were the second best days of our lives. What, we all wanted to know, were the best days of our lives? With a grin he replied, 'When you're not at school.'

I didn't realise it at the time, but he was right – there is a lot of fun in doing something other than what you are supposed to be doing. In industry, I soon discovered that the borderlands between what you were supposed to be doing and something else, were stimulating and untrodden, while my academic colleagues will tell you that I am still not very good at sticking to a discipline. However, there is danger in becoming too much of a non-specialist, since the experts on either side of the border will have a great view of your naivety.

But if you can risk the odd spectacular mistake, I commend the meander along the edge of your expert knowledge. The view is generally exhilarating and you sometimes catch sight of something that the others have missed. And that is about the best explanation I can give for attempting an oblique look at Daniel. I hope you enjoy the view.

I have some idea of the massive mismatch between my background and the book I have chosen to study, and if you want an expert opinion, you will need to find an expert. In mitigation, I have tried to dodge most of the tricky stuff and am grateful to a number of people who have helped me out. Bill Cotton reviewed an early draft and helped to eliminate some of the more serious gaffes. I picked up a helpful perspective on the beasts and the Lamb from Robert Gordon. Thank you both.

Beth Dickson took over from Harold Rowdon when the manuscript was in an advanced state – which provides me with the opportunity to thank two commissioning editors instead of one. Harold Rowdon, as usual, has been a great support, and has continued to produce thoughtful comments, especially in his careful way with detail. I owe him a debt of gratitude, not just for his work on this manuscript, but for the way in which he has helped me to become an author in the first place. Moving on, I would like to thank Beth for her willingness to pick up someone else's project and also for the thoughtful way in which she has helped to identify a passage here or there that could be polished or refined. The discussion has been fun and her contribution has, I believe, made a marked improvement to the content and flow. Where I have revisited the text, I have made emendations without altering allusions or illustrations in the adjacent passages – so the chronology may seem to jump about, once in a while.

Needless to say, my greatest debt is to Danielle and the boys for their forbearance over the last few years, and for that I do not think I can express sufficient thanks.

Datchet, 2006

Introduction

Daniel is a book full of bright, vivid stories that we remember from Sunday school. There are stunning statues, dropped into Nebuchadnezzar's sleep or coated in gold for everyone to worship. Who could forget Daniel's three friends, tossed by an irate tyrant into the flames, or Daniel himself waiting patiently for dawn in a den of lions? And then there are the visions full of unbelievable creatures that stalk the earth and guzzle all opposition before being destroyed by the next beast to come along.

Despite the fact that many of the stories make it into our childhood curriculum, interpreting the book is a controversial business. Many scholars reject the notion that Daniel was written at the time the events are reported. The critical view is that Daniel's legend was committed to writing a couple of centuries down the line, when the Jews were suffering back in their homeland under a particularly nasty tyrant. On this reading, the visions are a literary device in which the author's history is presented as Daniel's future in an attempt to bring hope to a hopeless situation.

Nonetheless, the visions and prophecies, particularly in the second half of the book, have long been believed to provide a complicated set of clues about the future – our future, even. From his perspective, Jesus believed that Daniel still had something to say about the future. The exercise of combining the predictions made by Jesus with those of Daniel and of John in the book of Revelation, has generated a mass of literature that presents a formidable barrier to anyone wanting to contribute to this field.

I have to state that I am ill equipped to address these issues formally, and so I hope to find a way to sneak around them and find a way into Daniel for the non-specialist. For those wanting to review the contentious issues, I would recommend the IVP commentaries as a useful place to start. My IVP commentary on Daniel was written by Joyce Baldwin (see Bibliography), but they are periodically reviewed, and your copy may have been written by someone else. I always enjoy the first hundred pages or so of these commentaries and the generally conservative analysis resonates with my take on scripture.

So let's move on. What can a non-expert, who is neither historian nor theologian, bring to the study of Daniel? Well, perhaps I can encourage you simply to read the book! The Old Testament is neglected these days, a situation that can only worsen as long as we believe that Daniel is somehow territory fit only for children (the stories) or experts (the visions). I hope I can persuade you that you can get into the book, deepen your worship and learn from Daniel without needing to get on top of all the difficulties that Daniel presents.

Beyond that, I think there are some aspects of Daniel's life, particularly his working life, which would not appeal to the traditional commentator, but may be worth some scrutiny here. The thing that excites me about Daniel is how recognisable he is as a senior player at work. I am fascinated by the way he responds to challenges, negotiates with skill and recovers seemingly impossible situations. Such skills are highly prized today. Anyone in the workplace will appreciate Daniel's command of that environment.

I do not want to overstate the case, but this ring of reality in the narrative presents a mystery for me if the book was written, many years later, by a scribe or prophet in Palestine. Management skills are hard enough to nurture with training and hard work. To discover them inadvertently incorporated into a text that was written for a completely different purpose would be, for me, quite amazing. As we shall see in chapter 5, someone like Ezekiel, for instance, would not have been able to identify such skills, let alone appreciate their impact or importance. From a workplace perspective, I am impressed at how well the narrative makes sense as it stands.

And it is from this perspective that I think Daniel has so much to offer us today. With the exile to Babylon, God's people moved into new territory. The old mould was broken and new precedents were being set. The fun in Daniel comes from watching how he will cope with a secular job, working alongside people whose world view is different from, and sometimes hazardous to, his own. And I hope that, for many Christians, this will provide a fruitful and helpful way into the book.

But I am also dissatisfied with the way we normally split the book. The book itself has some interesting textual divisions, which I am not equipped to comment on, but even in our translations, we tend to split the stories from the visions. This leaves us with two half-books, one of which contains striking stories that we hand on to our children, and the other which contains perplexing pictures that we leave with the scholars. There does not seem to be much left for ordinary people. I want to find a foothold in Daniel that works for grown-ups and enables them to emerge with a blessing from the exercise.

Clearly, this involves parking some of the more difficult issues. As I say, if you want to follow them up, there are plenty of places to look for information – but this isn't one of them. If you can do that, this book may have something to say to you.

Great and small

So what happens if we park the problems of background, text, and how and when the book was written, and try to address the narrative as a whole? I believe a number of themes emerge that are critical to our day because the book manages to connect two important levels of reality, God in the little things, and God over the whole world. At first sight, the book is about a displaced person and his friends and the way that God looks after them. The first challenge is to discover whether the God they worship is big enough to protect them beyond their homeland border. Has Daniel any right to expect that his beliefs are more than a personal or local phenomenon? In a raw and chilling way, Daniel and his friends are exposed to a world where Yahweh is not recognised by the vast majority. In fact it looks like Yahweh may well be a minor player in a game that is dominated by the big boys. Didn't the gods of Babylon demonstrated their supremacy in a devastatingly destructive display and finally leave Jerusalem in ruins. Aren't they the ones driving the exiles on their despondent way to Babylon? The first surprise to the neutral observer is that God is able to look after Daniel and his friends.

However, another theme starts to play out in which God reveals himself to Nebuchadnezzar as the God of heaven (Dan 2:37) and begins to make an impact in Babylon. The story develops from there with more dreams and visions that are clearly global in nature. From here on, the camera keeps switching between the micro-scale of individual people and the macro-scale of nations. Understanding how these connect together – the personal and the global – is perhaps the most important insight Daniel has to offer. Daniel is happy to carry a personal faith into an indifferent, and occasionally hostile world, but that is not enough. It is not enough that Daniel's faith works for Daniel. What does it say about the rest of the world? Well, the message of Daniel is that the God who meets with and protects individuals is also God over the nations. I hope you enjoy the interplay as you read on.

Unfolding the book

During the first three chapters, I hope we can examine the way in which Daniel finds his feet and prospers under Nebuchadnezzar. After considering his traumatic arrival in chapter 1, we go on to study Daniel as a manager and to observe his skills in the workplace. Chapter 3 takes this theme further by remembering that Daniel has a series of careers, first as a senior civil servant, then as a visionary and finally in intercessory prayer for his nation. Throughout these chapters, I hope we can identify some helpful resonances that connect Daniel's day with our own, especially as the jobs-for-life paradigm collapses and people expect to have several careers in a lifetime. An interesting question is whether one of those careers should involve an overtly Christian ministry.

Broadening focus, we consider the impact God is planning on the monarch himself in chapter 4. Why should God want to forge a relationship with Nebuchadnezzar? Daniel's story reminds us that God is interested in big people as well as little people and the tussle between Nebuchadnezzar and God is an absorbing reminder that God has global interests.

The next three chapters (5, 6 and 7) consider visionaries and the visions. I hope the dual perspective of local detail against global sweep will help to tie these to the earlier stories. Even the dreams have this stylistic clash: Daniel's earlier dreams contain vivid pictures depicting broad themes, while his last is just numbing detail. Continuing this theme to its conclusion in chapter 7, we look at the scriptural predictions about the end of all time.

Chapter 8 considers Daniel's final career-move into a life of prayer for his nation and we consider how this ministry might apply to us today. The last chapter tries to pull it all together with a snapshot from the end of the prophecy.

Retreating to victory

As I try to stand back I am reminded of my Mom, who had a way of retreating to victory with my Dad. She didn't always manage it, but the strategy went something like this. Mom would decide that something was needed around the house – perhaps a new carpet or a side table. Dad would explain that they couldn't afford it, did not really need it, or should give the money to someone in greater need. My Mom would gently agree and then, a few weeks later you would walk in, and there it would be, as large as life! Despite all the reasons why it should not have been bought, and without countering any of them, Mom would win the day and reach her objective.

In a sense, Daniel is a case of retreating to victory. It looks like Yahweh has encountered a terrible setback that might be fatal. The nation that received God's special blessing has been conquered and deported. And yet, from the ashes of this disaster emerges a greater triumph, a much greater triumph. But it comes not from defeating the host community, but by being absorbed into it.

The heart of Christianity is alive to this paradox. It is the corn of wheat that dies, which provides the rich harvest. And in the supreme example of retreating to victory, it is the crucified Nazarene who returns as the risen Lord of all. A favourite snatch of an old hymn catches the theme:

By weakness and defeat He won the meed and crown;
Trod all our foes beneath his feet by being trodden down.

(Whitlock Gandy)

I hope you find this a stimulating way into Daniel that takes you a little way off the beaten track. I hope you find something for your personal walk with God, and that you are also encouraged at what is happening around the world. But it's your call from here.

Enjoy…

1

Pond life

The book of Daniel opens with a scene of destruction and despair. 'In the third year of the reign of Jehoiakim king of Judah, Nebuchadnezzar king of Babylon came to Jerusalem and besieged it. And the Lord delivered Jehoiakim king of Judah into his hand, along with some of the articles from the temple of God. These he carried off to the temple of his god in Babylonia and put in the treasure-house of his god' (Dan 1:1,2).

The prophet Jeremiah sees the destruction coming, but even so his heart is broken at the mess that follows from being on the wrong side of conquest. In the book of Lamentations, a solemnly sad set of carefully constructed songs, he gives us a feel for the abject hopelessness of it all. Take the following snatch, for instance:

> Young and old lie together in the dust of the streets;
>   my young men and maidens have fallen by the sword.
> You have slain them in the day of your anger;
>   you have slaughtered them without pity.
> As you summon to a feast day,
>   so you summoned against me terrors on every side.
> In the day of the LORD's anger no one escaped or survived;
>   those I cared for and reared, my enemy has destroyed.
>
> (Lam 2:21, 22)

Although the narrator clearly believes that God, the God of Israel, is still in control, it would not have looked that way to most objective observers. It would certainly not have appeared that way to Nebuchadnezzar. The rule with gods was simple – armies supported by powerful gods trashed armies that worshipped weaker gods. The winner swept up the accoutrements of worship from the loser's temple and took them home to his own trophy cupboard of a temple. And that is the way it was.

To any rational observer, it must have looked like the end of the line for the God who first appeared to Abraham and then to Moses, who meandered with that uneasy crowd across the desert and found them a safe place to perch, where they clung to their hills between the Jordan and the sea. To begin with, of course, it had looked as if it would all work out. After a few centuries, they had extended their patch considerably and dominated the locals. However, the rot had set in, and a pedigree stretching back something like a millennium was finally about to be assimilated into something bigger, something grander, something more enduring. Something with its capital a long, long way away.

It must have been a shattering experience for Daniel and his friends (Dan 1:3-5) to watch the destruction and then to be taken away to the domain of this powerful deity. Today they would probably be accused of denial, of failing to see the obvious in the sequence of events and clinging vainly to a hope that God would somehow be able to look after them. Not only were they soon out of reach of the site where God had once been worshipped, but the whole framework of worship – the temple, the system of sacrifices, the rotas of priest and Levite – had been dismantled. Would God be able to exert any kind of influence in the new environment? Did the God they worshipped have the global reach to protect Daniel and his friends?

In a sense, this question forms the backdrop to the whole of Daniel. Starting as a refugee, the silver spoon well and truly wrenched from his mouth, we watch Daniel move into unknown territory. The great thrust of the book is not simply that he rises to prominence in this new world. It is not just that he is able to do what no-one else can do, or even that he is preferred above his peers in the deadly world of palace politics. Although the ways in which God protects his own is an amazing theme, the most surprising development for me is that God takes a hand in life at the palace, advising, directing and at times obstructing Nebuchadnezzar in his plans. And beyond that, we see God starting to reach across the globe and shake history with something new.

Back to square one

So let's try to imagine what it must have been like to have everything familiar wiped away in your teens. Although they had grown up under the shadow of Babylon, and while the siege years must have brought everyone low, Daniel and his friends had enjoyed the best of what was going. From their subsequent behaviour, we have to guess that they took their worship seriously, in contrast to the courtiers depicted by Jeremiah (e.g. Jer 32:32). Despite the anxieties, life revolved around some certainties. There was the comforting ritual of worship, a place to go and meet with God, and the voice of godly prophets able to make themselves heard occasionally above the sycophantic babble.

I wonder what Daniel's parents were like. Did they take a stand against the tide of godlessness and intrigue? Were they caught up in the power plays? There is so little we know about Daniel's family before the capital fell, and there is not much sign of any family afterwards. Did Daniel become a eunuch in the court of Nebuchadnezzar? Who knows? Whatever his parents' role in life, there were elements of his upbringing that must have prepared Daniel for a life ahead.

In many ways, Daniel's story runs parallel to that of Joseph centuries earlier – wrenched away from his family in his late teens (Gen 37:2,12-36) to a completely foreign culture. Although he would probably have known the story, nothing can have prepared him for the shock of exile. All the promises of the land, made first to Abraham and fulfilled through Moses and Joshua – gone. The city of the Great King (Psa 48:2), where God had agreed in a special way to live among his people – trashed. The people who had formed the bedrock of that society – dead or heading for exile.

So how will Daniel, a young, and suddenly very insignificant person, survive the rough road into exile? The first chapter of Daniel describes how Daniel's personal position is assured. The conquerors have a system for integrating the best of the rest into their own society, and Daniel and his friends are chosen for three-year apprenticeships in the king's service. There is the tricky matter of not wanting to defile themselves through what they ate – and we will want to come back to this. Apart from Daniel's faithfulness to God throughout, we see two other ingredients in Daniel's success. First, God blesses him with special gifting in an area that really matters in Babylon – the interpretation of dreams. Second, Daniel benefits from his upbringing. He has had a great education; he has been nourished in times of want; he is used to the ways of palaces and has settled readily into the routine. And so, when we bring all this together, Daniel and his friends waltz through their viva and the king is impressed. He is just a small blip on Nebuchadnezzar's radar screen, but he is there.

The narrative gives us no idea of how Daniel coped with the impact of exile. Perhaps he understood that this was part of a national punishment. Maybe this helped him keep his cool in difficult times. However he coped, there is no evidence of rancour or anger. Neither do we get the picture of a man who has bottled up his emotions. Somehow Daniel has come to terms with his new environment and manages to move on.

So the first phase of his rehabilitation is complete – Daniel is out of immediate danger, he has a role in life and a recognised position in Babylon.

But what about the pain and abuse?

Can Daniel really put behind him all the cruelties of the invasion and the miseries of the road? Daniel appears to have been an early casualty of the conflict and to that extent, missed the worst. The first phase of defeat was to create a vassal state in which the elite were taken to Babylon, partly perhaps as hostages, partly for the enrichment of the master empire, partly for their own social and career development. However, let us be under no illusions about life in defeat. This is the same Nebuchadnezzar who took king Zedekiah, slaughtered his sons in front of him and then put out his eyes before shackling him in bronze for the rest of the journey to Babylon (2 Kings 25:1-7). Daniel's road to exile was probably a privileged pathway, especially compared to those who followed. In due course, there were those who were deemed less significant, and the Psalmist paints a desperate picture of slaughtered infants (Psa 137:9). Meanwhile Obadiah watches fugitives, caught at the crossroads by the Edomites, being handed over to the invaders (Obad 14). Terror, outrage, cruelty.

Nor is the humiliation over when he arrives in Babylon. There he is given a new name, Belteshazzar (Dan 1:7) as part of an exercise to wash away his old identity and reinvent him as a Babylonian in a new society. I doubt if we can easily gauge the treatment Daniel received, or the extent to which he was aware of the horrors experienced by his less favoured countrymen. On the one hand, he was well treated by the standards of his day. By our standards he had a harrowing time of it. Whatever Daniel does, however, life has become more precarious – the journey, the palace, the politics.

As Western Christians, we are slowly coming to believe that we can never escape the scars of scorching circumstances. We are increasingly convinced that the things that have happened to us have an indelible, inescapable impact. Today, counsellors would have flocked to advise and support Daniel and his friends. He would have been encouraged to talk over the worst of his nightmares, to articulate his feelings towards each and every guard he met. He might well have emerged convinced that he had a grievance against his captors and against God himself. He might even have experienced counselling dependency.

Before you pigeon-hole me as a specialist in the stiff upper lip, or write me off as hopelessly opposed to any form of counselling, let us try and open up this problem.

First of all, I hope we can recognise that a Daniel full of reproach towards the God who has allowed this to happen could never have exercised the ministries he did, especially in interceding for his people. The whole fabric of the story is electric with Daniel's relationship with God. Without that trust in God, that dependence on divine leading, Daniel would never have survived at the palace, and it is doubtful whether he would ever have exhibited the sort of attitude that allowed him to rise at all. Certainly, a Daniel seething silently at the Babylonians would never have advised Nebuchadnezzar as he did (Dan 4:19) and could never have been the conduit, ultimately, of God's blessing to this ruler.

If Daniel was to have any chance of a fruitful ministry, therefore, he had to learn to leave the past behind. The question of how, might prove more difficult. But there could be no question of whether. Paul catches something of the same need: 'But one thing I do: Forgetting what is behind and straining toward what is ahead, I press on toward the goal to win the prize for which God has called me heavenward in Christ Jesus' (Phil 3:13b, 14).

And I am concerned at times to see Christians who believe they have a right to be angry. They have a right to feel distressed about the past. As a third-party observer, I sometimes wonder if their counselling encourages them to return too often and ruminate too frequently on the past. Sometimes, I cannot help feeling that they risk carrying greater distress into the future than they inherited from past. Sometimes their ministry is straitened, warped and withered in consequence, often in ways that they can never see because the opportunities to take a very different path can never open before them while they are so absorbed with the past. What if Daniel the malcontent had spent his life regretting those early years, never making it at court, never developing a ministry of his own, never learning to pray for his people? It would be hard to track that back, in any sort of logical way, to his attitude. And yet, looking at Daniel from this perspective, we can see how crippling his past could have been had he not learned to deal with it. The palace was a dangerous place for anyone with a chip on his shoulder.

Having said that, we must recognise the value of clinical counselling, for instance, in treating mental illness. As I understand it, there are reproducible beneficial outcomes from clinical counselling. In his book, *Happiness: Lessons from a New Science*, Richard Layard presents some fascinating evidence on how well we can measure the state of happiness in individuals and societies around the world. From the evidence, he makes a strong case for counselling – and I am open to those arguments.

We must also recognise that Churches have, in the past, discounted mental illness and applied disciplinary or other measures in ways that have not helped and have often harmed. However, it seems to me that the pendulum is swinging the other way. To switch metaphors in mid paragraph, there is a counselling bandwagon careering through our churches. The knee-jerk reaction that anyone with an adverse experience automatically needs counselling, seems to me to take it too far. People are fundamentally robust, and find many strategies to cope with disaster. Counselling may well be a part of one's strategy – and it may not.

I recently reviewed some research assessment criteria for a research-funding agency and found, to my horror, that it was regarded as a bonus if a piece of research led to further research. To my mind, this was a licence for researchers to print money. Write proposals for research that will lead to more proposals for research! Surely one of the aims of research is to close down some questions and to reach a conclusion – not always, but once in a while. And I feel there is an element of this to the current counselling scene. It is becoming a self-perpetuating industry.

Matthew Parris wrote a column in The Times recently bemoaning our societal tendency to seek refuge from the stresses of everyday life in retreats. He advocated the opposite – advances, he called them – where you get up early and work hard all day. And for some that may be the answer – a bit more energy, a bit less focus on self.

Finally, in my very limited experience, I have come across those who have not emerged completely healed, although they have acquired a framework of reference for their problem. This new set of terms and concepts, however, does not equate to having dealt fully with the past. In extreme cases the new framework and language may even provide them with the techniques to justify their position and manipulate those around them.

So, where does that leave us? Perhaps your experience of counselling has been a great help. Maybe, with some catastrophe to deal with, you have sought counselling and emerged with a richer faith and a freedom from the past. If so, great! However, if it hasn't worked for you, or if someone you are trying to support is not being helped in this way, there are some ideas that emerge from Daniel.

And how does Daniel come to terms with the shock of defeat, the atrocities of war and a world under muscular new management? Perhaps this question mattered much less in those days than it would today. And yet there is some evidence within the text of principles that worked for Daniel.

A circle of friends

If we are to read the book simplistically (and I am all for a simple reading of narratives), then the record stretches over many decades. Daniel's friends, Hananiah, Mishael and Azariah (who are given the Babylonian names Shadrach, Meshach and Abednego) feature prominently in the first few chapters (Dan 1:7). Daniel appears to be their spokesman in the negotiations over what food they should eat (Dan 1:11-16). They are mentioned as a foursome later on in the chapter (Dan 1:17) and are jointly commended in their final viva (Dan 1:19,20). It is to his three friends that Daniel returns, asking for support in prayer, when the king makes the impossible request that his wise men tell him his dream as well as its interpretation (Dan 2:17-19).

So part of the answer is that Daniel does benefit from counselling as he and his friends look after one another. Why do we not see more of this peer-to-peer support today? Part of the answer may be that we lack the depth of friendship that makes it possible. I wonder why. Population-churn as our careers follow the jobs? A preoccupation with material things at the expense of relationships? Remember the thorns in the story of the sower – the 'worries of this life and the deceitfulness of wealth' strangling the life out of the good seed (Matt 13:22)? Jesus makes another interesting observation about the end times when he says, 'Because of the increase of wickedness, the love of most will grow cold' (Matt 24:12). Ring true?

And so, perhaps we find ourselves seeking professional support because we lack the security of families as well as the infrastructure of longstanding friendships. To some extent, churches create this infrastructure through prayer triplets, home groups, cell groups, fellowships at college or universities – and many are very successful. I remember reading a snippet from Charles Swindoll on a calendar one morning, where he pointed out the benefit of having a group of Christians who hold one another accountable in their faith. It is a helpful discipline and takes the exercise beyond being a talk shop. Remember that bit in Hebrews – 'And let us consider how we may spur one another on toward love and good deeds' (Heb 10:24)? There is also a piece in Galatians where Paul sets a balance between what we can do for one another and what we must do for ourselves: 'Carry each other's burdens, and in this way you will fulfill the law of Christ… Each one should test his own actions. Then he can take pride in himself, without comparing himself to somebody else, for each one should carry his own load' (Gal 6:2,4,5).

In a different world, healthcare, the trend is to put the patient in control of his or her care delivery. Sometimes this means providing the housebound with a budget to buy in help. Sometimes it means opening up the appointment system to patient choice. But however one achieves it, it means putting the individual at the centre of the process and moving the expert to a supporting role. In Daniel's case this is exactly what happens. He must struggle with God over his problems but he does so in the knowledge that his friends are praying for him.

Daniel and his friends are an ideal example of such a group – they are peers, they have been through the same experiences and they have a desire to be faithful to their God whatever happens. And so it is not surprising that many counselling services seek, in some way, to get away from the therapist-patient model to a peer group model with self-help groups. In Daniel's case, the peer group provides enough support for each member, but the absence of an expert provides the motivation for each member to secure his own relationship with God. Notice this interplay between the corporate and the personal when Daniel is seeking the meaning of Nebuchadnezzar's dream. Daniel 'urged' his friends to 'plead', but it is Daniel to whom the mystery must be revealed (Dan 2:18,19).

I guess the nearest I have come to this type of friendship was through a leadership team at a church where I served for about a decade. However, I think it was only in the final 2-3 years that I appreciated the support of the others in the way I should have. This became very apparent when I went through a job change. Clearly, my wife and I had to make the decisions ourselves. However, others on the team offered specific pieces of support, from looking over business plans to circulating my CV. It was quite a moving time, too, as we were made to feel valued and loved. I discovered just how much I was appreciated on the team during those very uncertain months.

Daniel encourages us to seek fellowship amongst Christian peers – cue fellowships at educational establishments or work. My experience of the former has ranged from good to excellent, but I have not really found that workplace fellowships work for me. An exciting development in our days is the number of talented young people taking a year or two out of their careers and finding themselves in school-related work. Their energy, enthusiasm and sheer Christian zest is a wonderful blessing where there are the funds to support them. If nothing else, surely the first chapter of Daniel encourages us to put more of our resource into people to support these ministries and to encourage our churches to club together to promote and fund such activity.

Coming from the Christian Union at university, I guess I expected the fellowship at work to be similar. Perhaps I had changed. Perhaps the range of people, interests, maybe even their roles at work, combined to undermine real peer-to-peer interaction. Maybe there wasn't the time needed to develop a fourth dimension of existence – to add to the work itself, home life and church life. These days there are some really good books about being a Christian at work and Mark Greene in particular

has done much to promote the workplace as a context for worship and service, as well as a place for evangelism. But I am still
not sure we have cracked the bit about meeting at work. What
has worked for me has been the informal meeting, when I have
had one or two Christian colleagues in the same laboratory and
we have informally met to pray. More formal meetings involving people from across the organisation, with the occasional outside speaker, have not done it for me. Maybe I was never sure
what these events should have achieved. Maybe we weren't
under the sort of pressures that forced Daniel and his friends
together. Maybe we weren't peers in that sense. Maybe the
meetings were great for others. I can only relate that they did
not work for me. I feel that anyone able to make progress on this
front and help Christians working together to meet regularly
and to mutual benefit, would bring a great deal of blessing in
their wake.

One might even see this pattern in Daniel. It is a bit of a guess,
because the narrative is so sparse, but the circle of friendship
seems to have been at its strongest when they were in training
together. As they move on into the world of work, they clearly
stay in touch for a while, but they seem no longer to be a team.
Shadrach, Meshach and Abednego fade after chapter 3. Nor do
we see another team forming around Daniel that carries him
forward into the next phase of his life. I am not sure whether
that is an indication that the workplace fellowship isn't worth
going after, or that it just tells us it was pretty difficult back then,
too. Whatever the message, I find it generally cheering that
other people, especially such people as Daniel and his friends,
appear to have faced the same sort of difficulties that I have had.

However, I have been blessed with a few long-term friendships and I notice that they seem to go in cycles. There have
been periods where I have taken a lot from the friendship.
Sometimes there seem to have been years when I have looked
for encouragement and support before the cycle has changed
and I have had the privilege of giving back something of what I
have taken out. I have also noticed that there have been long
stretches where I have felt I was putting the greater effort into
maintaining contact before, again, the cycle has switched and
the other person has made the running, as situations have
changed in both our lives.

Help! What if I don't have those types of friendship? I don't know of any way to become a friend other than to make the effort. The business of friendship is in some danger in the UK, and we are not knee-deep in good role models as far as establishing long-term friendships is concerned. The news story in yesterday's media was the contrast between young people's perception of their greatest need, and their parents' prime concern. Parents cited drugs as their major worry. Their kids cited relationships as their biggie.

My parents were missionaries and felt that an open home was an essential part of their ministry, especially working in the Middle East where people are so hospitable. And so our home had a steady throughput of people – Arabs, Westerners, ex-pats from India, who were the mainstay of the commercial systems at the time, RAF and Army personnel from the local bases, plus passing missionaries needing a meal on their way inland, or a bed for the night and a lift to the airport. Most of our visitors were fun to have around. One or two were nuts. Some have remained friends with the family over the intervening decades. Some we never saw again.

When we returned to the UK, the scene was much the same, the variety of visitors, perhaps dampened by the weather in the West Midlands. Certainly this environment created many friendships across a range of races and backgrounds and almost 400 of them came to the funeral when my Dad died unexpectedly at 67.

Perhaps the most important heritage from my childhood was the realisation that your home, and particularly the meal table, is a great place for spawning friendships. Today our homes are showcases for our success and DIY prowess. Our expectations of the meals we should serve visitors are often impossibly elevated, and exercises that could have been good fun are reinvented as tough tests of our culinary skills. 'Do not forget to entertain strangers, for by so doing some people have entertained angels without knowing it' (Heb 13:2).

Maybe we are afraid of putting on a poor show. Maybe we feel that a proper event takes so much effort that we have to clear the decks well in advance. Whatever our worries, there is a great benefit for those who will take the risk, open up their lives and start forging friendships. Even if you feel you have missed the boat, you may be able to provide a model for the generation coming up.

And I am not sure I can offer much more help on that one. If you have the gift of throwing a meal together at short notice (or are married to someone who can); if you can share your time; if you can work around visitors; if you can be yourself while they are around and enable them to be themselves – make the most of it! You have the capacity to be a blessing to others while being blessed yourself.

While Daniel's friends clearly play an important role over those tumultuous and critical years – perhaps for even a decade – in the palace, there are at least two other important principles worth considering here. One probably influenced Daniel greatly, and while it is hard to know how aware he was of the other, it is certainly important to us in coming to terms with our past.

A sense of purpose

The first is Daniel's relationship with God and the sense of purpose this lends to his life. What is it they say? 'The sun that softens wax, hardens clay.' It is true in marriages. Tough circumstances seem either to drive a wedge between couples or to strengthen the bond to a point where it becomes unbreakable. Talk to anyone whose marriage has survived redundancy, home repossession, a serious problem with a child, or chronic illness.

For Daniel, the trip into exile is a crunch point in his relationship with God. For those of us who are not part of some tightly knit community, Daniel's corporate approach to God has unfamiliar corners. Daniel sees in his own experience not just God's personal dealing with him as an individual, but a shared experience as part of the Jewish nation. And the nation is being punished for its apostasy, its syncretism, its idolatry, its materialism, its treatment of the poor, and its determination to cut God out. Later on, we know that Daniel read Jeremiah's writings (Dan 9:2), but a straightforward reading of the text leaves open the possibility that Daniel knew of Jeremiah and his preaching as he was growing up. There can have been no clearer proclamation that judgement was coming because of national sin, but that restoration would follow with national repentance.

It is probably hard for us to get inside this set of beliefs, but it leaves Daniel with an understanding that the punishment is temporary. The hand of God may seem harsh, but that hand is still there. Harsher still would be its withdrawal. And so Jeremiah, having warned of impending judgement for years, can write to the exiled community encouraging it to settle down and seek the welfare of its host nation (Jer 29:1-23). God has not forgotten them.

Daniel is aware of this backdrop of national punishment and he is able, perhaps over decades, to identify with God's people in their punishment. The result is the remarkable prayer in chapter 9.

The fact that there is a purpose in all of this provides, paradoxically, reassurance to the exiled community, to Daniel and to his friends. But alongside the national purpose of punishment and restoration, Daniel must soon have become aware of a secondary, personal purpose for himself and his friends. For Daniel's experience carries two almost conflicting elements – national disaster, personal triumph. He is not the only exiled Jew to experience great success against a backdrop of national humiliation: Esther, Mordecai and Nehemiah make similar journeys.

Because God has a purpose for each of us we can look on our past, however painful or discouraging it may be, as a launch pad for the future. We catch some of this in Jeremiah's letter to the exiles – a widely quoted passage that has brought comfort to many. '"For I know the plans I have for you," declares the Lord, "plans to prosper you and not to harm you, plans to give you hope and a future"' (Jer 29:11). And hope goes with purpose.

As we shall see, the ability to keep his head under unreasonable pressure, to show loyalty to a foreign potentate, to accept that his star will sometimes wane on the horizon – all of these are elements in a puzzle. They help Daniel to discover that God is at work in Babylon and as he comes to understand each piece of this puzzle, he is able to play a part in God's initiative for Babylon.

So how can a belief that God has a purpose in the disasters we have encountered – how can that help us to deal with our past? Well, we need to realise that our lives are meant to bring glory to the God we worship. And in those lives we are not given a head start with endless ease or boundless blessings. There is a sense in which God is indiscriminate in blessing both the good and the bad, and disasters befall those who worship as well as to those who don't: 'Your Father in heaven… causes his sun to rise on the evil and the good, and sends rain on the righteous and the unrighteous' (Matt 5:45).

God wants to show to the world around that those who worship are able to overcome – a theme that runs through the book of Job. 'Then the LORD said to Satan, "Have you considered my servant Job? There is no one on earth like him; he is blameless and upright, a man who fears God and shuns evil. And he still maintains his integrity, though you incited me against him to ruin him without any reason"' (Job 2:3).

And out of such experiences comes an ability to help and support others. How does Paul write to his friends in Corinth? 'Praise be to the God and Father of our Lord Jesus Christ, the Father of compassion and the God of all comfort, who comforts us in all our troubles, so that we can comfort those in any trouble with the comfort we ourselves have received from God. For just as the sufferings of Christ flow over into our lives, so also through Christ our comfort overflows. If we are distressed, it is for your comfort and salvation; if we are comforted, it is for your comfort, which produces in you patient endurance of the same sufferings we suffer. And our hope for you is firm, because we know that just as you share in our sufferings, so also you share in our comfort' (2 Cor 1:3-7).

Part of the 'purpose' puzzle for us, then, is that by coming to terms with our past, we may develop a ministry towards others. Those who are able to grieve and emerge from grieving are best placed to support the bereaved. Those who have overcome prejudice are best able to support those currently going through the mill. The need to encounter God for real, to look to his strength and accept prayerful support from others – these are experiences that we can offer to others in their time of need.

A second element of the 'purpose' puzzle is that some aspects of our character cannot be developed without an element of suffering. 'In this [hope] you greatly rejoice, though now for a little while you may have had to suffer grief in all kinds of trials. These have come so that your faith – of greater worth than gold, which perishes even though refined by fire – may be proved genuine and may result in praise, glory and honour when Jesus Christ is revealed' (1 Pet 1:6,7). Patience is not acquired in a fortnight, humility is rarely a by-product of rapid promotion.

Is this still a tenable position today? Traditional Christianity, and perhaps particularly Catholicism, has long recognised the shaping role that suffering can play in our lives. Down through the centuries, faithful Christians have seen a providential hand behind their suffering. 'But he knows the way that I take; when he has tested me, I will come forth as gold' (Job 23:10). They have recognised that, while the suffering itself has not been good, God has been able to bring good out of it. Theories have still to settle down, but there is mounting evidence that prosperity brings many social and personal benefits – although as Richard Layard reports in his book on happiness, our explosive wealth creation in the West has not made us any happier of late. Nonetheless, social policy is being built around eliminating all forms of suffering and disadvantage from people's lives.

Clearly, Christian thinkers need to spend some time working through the concept of suffering in the light of unprecedented rises in prosperity around the globe. The idea that economic success is a key to heaven on earth is gaining credibility and, indeed, there is a great deal to commend it as such. Prosperity is likely to emerge as the great good and poverty as the great evil.

When the thinking has been done, I believe the Christian view of suffering will not be discarded as primitive nor as the strivings of a bygone age to accommodate the surrounding poverty. Rather, I believe we will see that some important aspects of character are still forged in the furnace of adversity. I was interested to see a newspaper article this past week that noted how many wealthy and successful people in this country still think of themselves as working class. Part of this may be the latest phase of the class war, but I think there is something else to it. I think many successful people recognise the struggles and deprivation of their early life as vital ingredients of their later success. In fact, it is amazing how many influential people have had to overcome some difficulty, illness or setback. I am not saying that a serious setback is essential to success, but it is amazing how often the pattern of later success involves early reverses or disadvantage.

The Christian angle on this is that God can use even the worst experiences to develop patience, to teach us to forgive, to break our brittleness and make us more accommodating people, and ultimately to teach us to depend on him. Certainly Daniel emerges from those early years with an utter dependence upon God, with patience, fortitude and a complete absence of rancour.

Forgiveness

Forgiveness is a concept that is not explicit in Daniel but is a very important New Testament principle for dealing with the past. An ability to forgive others is the key to an open relationship after someone has done us a great injustice. It frees us from continued intimidation and a desire for vengeance. However, real forgiveness is usually quite hard to offer.

Forgiveness was a core part of Jesus' teaching. 'For if you forgive men when they sin against you, your heavenly Father will also forgive you. But if you do not forgive men their sins, your Father will not forgive your sins' (Matt 6:14,15). Jesus lived by that credo at the most extreme moment of pain: 'Father, forgive them, for they do not know what they are doing' (Luke 23:34). In his last words, the martyr Stephen manages in the same spirit: 'Lord, do not hold this sin against them' (Acts 7:60).

Most of us put people capable of such holiness into a category of their own and continue to carry our grudges against the colleague who eased his or her burden into our lap and let us carry the blame; the partner who has cheated on us; or the thug who has deprived us of a son or daughter. Ironically, failure to forgive in the face of severe maliciousness is probably less of a problem to most of us than the many minor grievances we allow to accumulate, the grudges we nurse, and the relationships that harden close to hatred as a result.

I know it was a well-known story at the time, but Corrie Ten Boom's account of forgiving the guard from Ravensbruck is something that still illustrates both aspects of forgiveness today – that it is difficult but that it is not impossible for ordinary people. She tells the story of her imprisonment by the Nazis for harbouring Jews in Holland during the second World War in *The Hiding Place*, which was made into a film of the same name. When I was growing up, there was a comic-strip version of the book. I watched the film and read the comic strip – I'm afraid I wasn't really into books then.

Anyhow, having suffered and survived the brutalities of life in a concentration camp, Corrie emerges to get on with the rest of her life. As a speaker with a riveting story to tell, she finds herself in demand. It comes to a crunch when she encounters one of the guards from her past, who has been converted. Her struggle to forgive this man and her ultimate victory in being able to do so is, for me, a highlight of the whole story.

Jesus is so concerned that we, as his followers, learn to forgive, that he presents layer upon layer of teaching on the topic. As usual, Jesus is interested in presenting many reasons for behaving in this way, so that each of us can find a reason that fits. The story of the unmerciful servant (Matt 18:21-35) sets our wrongs against one another in the context of our position with God. Whatever others may have done to us is insignificant next to our trespasses against almighty God. This may seem hard for us to swallow, fixated as we are on our selves, our rights, our bodies and our outlook. But Jesus' perspective is that we cannot forgive if each of us believes himself or herself to be the most important person in our universe. However, if God can forgive, all other acts of forgiveness pale into insignificance. Paradoxically, all other acts of forgiveness are only possible because of God's great act of forgiveness.

To help us along, Jesus links our receiving forgiveness directly to our forgiving others: 'And when you stand praying, if you hold anything against anyone, forgive him, so that your Father in heaven may forgive you your sins' (Mark 11:25). As we appreciate the extent of our sin against God, as we face up to our own wrongdoing and ask for his forgiveness, we find part of the puzzle falls into place and we have a stronger motivation to forgive others.

A robust appreciation of our own insignificance is also part of our salvation. It's all part of the paradox that the door to true self-worth opens only as we recognise that we are completely insignificant. I read a wonderful quotation from G K Chesterton: 'Angels can fly because they take themselves very lightly.' Isn't that a wonderful take on forgiveness, too?

In another parable – the story of the Pharisee and the tax collector (Luke 18:10-14) – Jesus reminds us that our assessment of other people's sin is often very unlike God's take on the situation. Furthermore, the Pharisee, oozing conceit and self-satisfaction, is unable to be forgiven because he has no sense of need. Ironically, the tax collector, whose shortcomings are all too evident, has a sufficient sense of need to seek (and obtain!) the forgiveness he so badly wants. Finally, while the story of the talents is not primary about forgiveness (e.g. Matt 25:14-30), it illustrates all too clearly the debilitation of nursing a grudge over a long period.

Putting all this together, how tragic it would be to get to the end of our days, having nursed a grudge over something that ultimately didn't matter, while creating huge problems of attitude against ourselves in the end.

Of course, none of this is to say that forgiveness is easy. But difficult or easy is a separate question. The way in which we set about doing something that is necessary for our own spiritual lives will depend upon us, and our circumstances. The combination of good friends, plus prayer – which features prominently in Daniel's life and which we will explore later – should help us to make an excellent start.

But on what basis can we forgive someone else? A snatch of one of Paul's letters gives us a clue. 'Therefore, as God's chosen people, holy and dearly loved, clothe yourselves with compassion, kindness, humility, gentleness and patience. Bear with each other and forgive whatever grievances you may have against one another. Forgive as the Lord forgave you. And over all these virtues put on love, which binds them all together in perfect unity' (Col 3:12-14). We can forgive because we are forgiven. The fact that my sin is a greater problem than other people's is only helpful if there is a way of dealing with my sin – and there is. God can forgive me. If God can crack the difficult problem, it leaves me free to address the more minor issues.

Still, something as difficult as forgiveness is not a feat we can tackle on our own. We need God's help and will often need the support of friends as well. Specifically, there are some approaches to forgiveness that are likely to fail. The stoical approach where we grit our teeth and try to act as though we have forgiven, fails on two counts. We never really forgive, and we have the added problem of coping with a new tension between how we really feel and the way we are pretending to feel about that person.

The other way we sometimes try to forgive without really forgiving, is to talk down the offence. At first sight, this seems like adopting the insignificance argument. She probably didn't mean it. He had a headache that morning. While a truly Christian spirit will genuinely recognise the mitigating circumstances, forgiveness involves facing up to the offence in all its magnitude and frankly forgiving. The trouble with playing it down, is that it often plays itself up again later. Ever been in an argument and something pops up from years ago? Maybe against you, maybe you brought it up – but the fact that it has reappeared probably means it has not been truly forgiven.

On to maturity

So we find that Daniel emerges intact from a traumatic spell in his teens. He takes forward the benefits of his high birth. He is at ease in the palace, he can take a high-level view of things. But he has also learned to cope with the humiliation of captivity. We catch no sense of resentment, bitterness or ill will. In his negotiation, Daniel is always free to adopt a positive, co-operative stance. He can take the king's welfare genuinely to heart.

Two lessons here, and then we must move on. First, we can feel grateful rather than guilty for the talents, background, or blessings that we have enjoyed. We can be at ease with ourselves, even if our upbringing has been much more privileged than that enjoyed by others. Unless the circumstances are criminal, I suggest that we need not feel guilty about the wealth of our family. The real test is how we take things forward. The rider is, 'From everyone who has been given much, much will be demanded' (Luke 12:48).

God has a wonderful way of exploiting those skills, talents and even networks as we yield our lives to him. It is the ex-Pharisee, Paul, who grounds some of the most wonderful ideas in the New Testament upon some of the most deep and difficult parts of the Old. Even trivial things, such as Amy Carmichael's annoying brown eyes in a blue-eyed nation turn out to be a wonderful asset as a missionary in later years. She grows up in Northern Ireland and asks God to change her eyes to blue so that she can fit in and be like everyone else. However, her prayers are not answered. Years later, as a missionary in India, she runs into trouble. Her adversaries are sure they will find a woman from Northern Ireland in India even if she disguises herself, because of her blue eyes. But, of course, her eyes do not expose her. Her disguise holds and she slips through the net and on to further service.

I don't know what skills or blessings you bring from your past to your present, or how you value them, but God has a use for even the most unlikely. He may even have special plans for those you would rather discard. I think of a friend of mine who became a Christian in his early forties. Most of his life-decisions seemed to have been behind him and, as a building site foreman, you might have thought there was little for him to do in Christian service. However, as he went on in his faith, he was drawn into running a hostel for down-and-outs. He had had a lifetime managing men, rough men, and was a big chap himself – which turned out to be key to his new ministry. He really understood the chaps who came into the hostel. He knew when they were trying it on and when they had needs beyond their ability to cope. And he made an impact in a very needy city.

On the negative side, and this is the second lesson, we may arrive at maturity (or an age when we ought to be mature) with scars from the past. The friends and forgiveness approach outlined above may free us from our past, but it may not always leave us as we would otherwise have been.

So what about us?

How about you and me? Have we made it without scars? Have we reached a mature adulthood with the freedom and drive to serve God usefully in our lives? And if we have not, how will we ever tell? I'm not sure that Daniel's story helps us to answer such questions – although it reminds us very powerfully of how important it is to grow into a mature child of God.

My own experience is that we carry forward greater strengths and weaknesses than we imagine. As a physically handicapped youngster brought up in a home where my parents determined that life should go on as normal as far as possible, life up until about 25 was a struggle. It was an exhilarating struggle because I usually won. Targets I set were almost always hit and while it sometimes took a while to get into my stride (so to speak), I was relentless thereafter.

There were, of course, a great many influences for good upon my life apart from the commitment of my parents and the forbearance of my siblings. A couple of teachers spotted potential and put the odd piece of unusual homework my way. One was almost certainly responsible for getting me through the 11+ and into the normal state school system. Having just spent some time in looking at 11+ papers with my own boys, I am amazed that I got through knowing so little. I guess I had always been a bit out of it, having lived abroad for much of my childhood, and we had only been in the UK for a few months when I took a day out from the special school I attended to sit the exam. I remember one question asking for two of the Prime Minister's pastimes. I knew Edward Heath was into sailing but nothing of his passion for music – and I had to let another point go down the drain.

However, there were enough points to send me to the local grammar school where there was a whole new world of people who revised for exams. I found that revision was good for me, too, but it still took two years before I came top of the class. After that we got shuffled around and I didn't dominate across the board again – although I made some bright friends whom I have kept to this day.

The great thing about being bright was that you could compete. The old 'O' levels and 'A' levels went down pretty well and I got a first at university. When my PhD viva was over, I had begun to realise that the 'challenges' were over. Nobody was going to set up more skittles for me to knock down.

And I thought I had made it through to manhood in excellent shape. On the whole I did not resent being disabled, and I certainly did not think anyone owed me a living. I still don't. In fact, one of those brainy friends from the class I could never come top of sent me some material on the thalidomide story. He is a doctor, had a professional interest in it and was quite upset at the way the drug had been marketed. I have never had a satisfactory explanation for why I am the shape I am. When my Mom was coming home in her first trimester with me, she was given something on the ship for seasickness. I have never tried to track the ship and the brief investigations made when I was in my teens put the medical opinion against my being thalidomide. My wife and I did some follow-up before we had the boys, but nothing was conclusive, although, again the medical opinion was against thalidomide.

I'm open-minded, myself. If I was a thalidomide child, then I am at the top end of the age range. However, I realised early on that it was not the sort of consuming question that was likely to bring happiness, and I think I got that right, too. So I had a sort of interest in the story. As I read, I realised I must have a strange take on life because I wasn't upset. I was working in industrial research at the time, and part of me could identify with the irresponsible 'can-do' attitude of a team determined to bring its dream solution to market. And yet part of me also recognised the appalling consequences. Where was I coming from? Perhaps I was just cynical over everyone else's 20:20 hindsight.

There had been signs that my success had an unwanted side effect in the form of a poor view of others. Not of everyone, you understand, but I had (still have) a way of being rubbed up the wrong way by others and of irritating them. My know-it-all attitude would send my Dad ballistic at times. I had a teacher who would take time out (unnecessarily, I thought) to take me down a peg or two. However, at the time, the solid successes were piling up faster than the soft failures.

It was working life that showed me that gritty independence only gets you so far. I realised that an iron will might propel an individual, but was a poor team motivator, unless accompanied by exceptional interpersonal skills, or exercised in an unyielding environment. Also, it sat ill alongside my other characteristics, such as taking a personal interest in staff development, or wanting to have fun at work.

I remember sitting at a management training event that started to catalyse much of this analysis for me, when the rest of the team suggested that I might be in denial over my disability. Denial? How can you forget about something that makes almost every move an effort, that has your mind racing ahead to plan ahead every moment of every day. How can you ignore something that costs sweat and, on occasion, every ounce of determination you possess, simply to keep up and make a pass at normality?

In the end, I realised that I had carried more into being a grown-up than I had imagined. The worst bits needed special care to ensure that relationships were not wrecked by being driven remorselessly or by a lack of sympathy for the weakness of another. And the best bits made me more unusual than I had really appreciated. And whatever I was, God was able to use it.

And it's probably the same for you. You may well have sharp edges and soft spots of which you may still be blissfully unaware. You may have yet to appreciate the true greatness of your gifts, especially if you have decided that they lie in unspectacular terrain.

While introspection can be a great blessing if applied in moderation, the real value of a character like Daniel is as an exemplar – someone against whom we may compare ourselves. He emerges from a very difficult experience with the wisdom, humility and good cheer to bring real benefit to his fellow men, and to reflect a glory to his God.

Thinking it through

1. Your church is concerned about the pastoral support on offer. Two initiatives have been identified: to create a pastoral team or to encourage people into prayer triplets. As part of this exercise, you are asked to assess the costs and benefits of prayer triplets. Given Daniel's experience, what guidelines might you suggest for setting up the prayer triplets?

2. Why do you think Daniel accepts a new name but not the king's menu?

3. If you were setting up a fellowship for Christians at your workplace, what goals would you set?

4. How can you tell if your life has reached a stage of maturity where it can be used to help your fellows and bring glory to God?

5. A single mother starts attending your Sunday morning service, having first encountered people from the church at your toddlers event on a Tuesday morning. You get talking one morning and she pours out a horrific tale of early rejection and an ongoing saga of violence from her boyfriend. You invite her to your home for coffee the next morning. You want to help, but feel that her experience is so different from your own that you are more likely to botch things up rather than to be a blessing. How would you pray and plan for the visit?

6. Think of three people who have made a big impact on your life. List one characteristic or gift that they share with each other, and one that each has possessed but the other two have lacked. Which of these would you most like to pass on to someone else?

7. What is the most privileged aspect of your upbringing? List three ways in which God has already used it to bless others?

8. Think of the person you find it most difficult to forgive. What makes it so hard to forgive that person? In what ways will withholding forgiveness wreck your own life? Think up two strategies that might help you to reach a position of forgiving that person?

9. Do Christians in this country suffer for the sins of the

society in which they live? If so, how? If not, why not?

10. What aspects of Daniel's story align well with modern counselling practice and which run counter to it?

11. How much of our effort should we put into trying to alleviate suffering in the world? Which tasks that Jesus set his followers would be easier in an anxiety-free world and which would be more difficult?

12. Your young and newly appointed pastor has just had an unpleasant blow-up with several people at church. You discover that he had a blow-up with the principal during his seminary training, although it did not surface when he was interviewed for this job. You re-read his references and note a cautious tone in two out of the five you took up. How would you determine whether this is a recurring problem or just a set of unfortunate conflicts?

2

Something on the workplace

One of the most intriguing things about Daniel is his ability to negotiate difficult circumstances. Whether he is trying to change the menu (Dan 1:8-16) or arrange a stay of execution (Dan 2:15,16) for himself and his colleagues, Daniel seems able to create a trusting and open environment with those who are at best disinterested in his fate, and at worst hostile towards him. In this chapter, we will try to look at some of the issues Daniel encounters in his working life.

Conflict had certainly been part of Daniel's earlier existence at the palace in Jerusalem, and indeed, the Israelites had always known warfare beyond their borders as well as spasms of cruel internal struggle. The Psalms are full of cries to God against unjust harassment, deadly enemies and overwhelming foes. However, with Daniel and his fellow exiles, a new dimension emerges. Before, even when the framework was a little warped, there was still a sound moral fabric underneath society that most people understood. This created a shared moral perception and a clear right-wrong divide. The story of David and Saul had introduced real ambiguities as David took hold of God's promise to him of eventual kingship but refused resolutely to take matters into his own hands (e.g. 1 Sam 24:3-7; 26:5-11). On the whole, however, if your conscience was clear, you could appeal to God for protection and help.

But there is a new wind blowing across the world that Daniel faces. He cannot make his appeal around right and wrong in the same way. The purposes of God, so important to the Jews, are unlikely to carry any weight in this new world. Things that would matter to the conscientious Jew are irrelevances around here. Would it be worth risking everything in this new culture over issues that the new neighbours were unlikely even to understand? How would you determine what mattered and what could be left aside? Would there be any scope for dialogue across the spiritual and moral divide that separated the exiles from their neighbours?

And this is one of the reasons I have so much time for Daniel. Most talks about Christian behaviour are essentially talks about Christian behaviour in church. Ethical dilemmas, when addressed at all, have been so sanitised and simplified as to be useless. Sermons are delivered without any apparent insight into the practicalities of a working environment where people are increasingly unlikely to share your beliefs. So how on earth is one to determine when to bend with the wind and when to risk the chop?

Daniel is a really exciting read because those are exactly the issues he faces. That is the sort of world Daniel arrives in. Perhaps the most encouraging thing about Daniel is that there is no 'us and them' in the end. God is God of the whole world. He will intervene in Nebuchadnezzar's court just as in David's court – more so, perhaps, than in the courts of many of the Jewish kings. People's backgrounds are much less important in this surprising view of the world, and God's power to touch lives anywhere, no matter how they have been trained or conditioned, is one of the great messages of Daniel.

Working it out

It seems to me that Christians in a secular environment have traditionally adopted one of two extreme stances. On the one hand they join in with everything that goes on at work so that, like the pigs and the farmers in George Orwell's *Animal Farm*, they become indistinguishable from those around them. The other crowd seem to set their faces against everything that happens in the workplace. The joy they exhibit on Sundays evaporates overnight and their influence during the rest of the week is decidedly negative.

Daniel avoids these extremes in a much harsher environment than most of us will ever encounter. What if your boss told you he had had a wonderful idea for the new brand launch over the weekend but he forgot it in the shower this morning? He wants you to tell him what his idea was and produce a plan detailing how to implement it and, by the way, if you can't... Well, he isn't going to fire you. He is going to execute you! You remember briefly that last product launch where everyone pretended they got it, hired in a pride of consultants and missed the whole point. You note wryly that it will not happen this time. Only those who really understand the game will be able to produce an effective analysis. Extreme? Not in Daniel's world.

The death-or-glory style of management can yield terrific results. Alexander the Great achieved near-miraculous results at the challenge of cracking open castles and citadels. Of course, he had more than one way to motivate his men, but there is a nice death-or-glory example that I first heard in a radio play and then followed-up in Robin Lane Fox's biography (where I finally found it on p 315 of the paperback edition!). On the trail of some rebels, Alexander and his army approached a nearly impregnable fortress in the Koh-i-nor mountains. The leadership laughed at his attempts to negotiate a surrender, and told him that if he wanted to come in, he would need troops with wings. He sought out 300 volunteers with mountaineering experience and put an attractive package of incentives together. Four years' Asian service would normally earn a soldier a talent, but twelve talents were on offer that night to the first climber to scale the cliff face. The other bonuses would be scaled down on this grand bonus, depending on each soldier's place in the race to the top. Under cover of darkness, 270 heroes pegged and pulled their way to the top. The next morning, their general was able to point to his men, perched impossibly above the fortress, and persuade the opposition that it was time to surrender. That night, however, 30 climbers paid the price, and daylight found them buried deep in the snow below.

Maybe, less savagely, you recognise something of this environment. What are the options? Macho overload, knowing that if you blink, you are finished? Caving in to life as a doormat? Keeping your own counsel, leaving no hostages to fortune? There is no evidence of arrogance in Daniel, although he gets a little testy with Belshazzar (Dan 5:17-22). However, he is nobody's fool either, nor does he keep himself to himself. Somehow, Daniel manages to conduct himself with dignity and humility, to maintain open relationships with those whose world view differs radically from his own, and even with those who have authority to terminate his own existence. Through it all, he finds a narrow path that covers his conscience without treading on too many of the taboos of his host nation. A narrow path…

There used to be a chap called Bob at a church I went to in my late teens and early twenties, in many ways a very ordinary member of the congregation. I think he was a toolmaker. I don't know whether it was the focus at his lathe, or whatever, but there was a bit of a philosopher in Bob and his extempore contributions to the services were always rich with insights. I think many of them were lost on much of his audience, which felt he had a tendency to 'go on a bit'. I remember his take on the broad and narrow roads. 'Enter through the narrow gate. For wide is the gate and broad is the road that leads to destruction, and many enter through it. But small is the gate and narrow the road that leads to life, and only a few find it' (Matt 7:13,14).

Most readers will be aware of the traditional way of understanding this passage, in which Jesus is saying something about the difficulty and unpopularity of following his path. However, Bob saw that the path might be narrow for other reasons, too. He could see that it might be narrow because it had to wind its way between much easier extremes. And this, I think is a secret to Daniel's success. So how does he do it?

Conflict resolution

There are several occasions in which questions of faith bring Daniel or his friends into conflict with those around him – most of these stories are Sunday school favourites:

- the question of diet (Dan 1:8-16);
- avoiding execution along with the other wise men (Dan 2:1-16);
- worshipping the golden image (Dan 3);
- the prayer ban (Dan 6).

The latter are wonderful illustrations of a key approach to conflict – overt refusal to engage in behaviour that offends one's conscience. Daniel's friends refuse to prostrate themselves before the king's golden image, presumably in order not to violate the first and second commandments (Exod 20:1-4). Their non-compliance with the king's command is presumably low-key at first but, when they are denounced by some astrologers (Dan 3:8-12), they decline the king's direct invitation to comply (Dan 3:16-18).

In his own struggle with his peers over the issue of worship, Daniel carries on with his devotions as he has always done (Dan 6:10). In both cases, the exiles know that their behaviour is likely to attract the ultimate sanction. Interestingly, neither story concludes in martyrdom, although a martyr's death has been the lot of many who have defied the law before and since.

Shadrach, Meshach and Abednego put their case clearly: 'O Nebuchadnezzar, we do not need to defend ourselves before you in this matter. If we are thrown into the blazing furnace, the God we serve is able to save us from it, and he will rescue us from your hand, O king. But even if he does not, we want you to know, O king, that we will not serve your gods or worship the image of gold you have set up' (Dan 3:16-18).

We may add to this Jesus' own teaching: 'I tell you, my friends, do not be afraid of those who kill the body and after that can do no more. But I will show you whom you should fear: Fear him who, after the killing of the body, has power to throw you into hell. Yes, I tell you, fear him' (Luke 12:4,5). 'I have told you these things, so that in me you may have peace. In this world you will have trouble. But take heart! I have overcome the world' (John 16:33).

Take it or leave it

The central teaching of Scripture is that, at the end of the day, we have only our lives to lose, and that there is a world far more real than this, where the sacrifice will seem insignificant. I was recently given the topic of Stephen, the first Christian martyr, for a Sunday morning talk. I realised as I let the story roll around in my head that I was totally unqualified to give a talk on martyrs. And then I brightened up a little because I realised that, actually, there were no speakers able to talk authoritatively on the topic. Martyrs simply aren't around to talk about it afterwards.

The pattern with Stephen (Acts 6,7) was not dissimilar to the stories of Daniel and his friends that we find here. He doesn't seek the role. Rather, he feels he is unable to avoid it. This, of course, distinguishes a Christian concept of martyrdom from other flavours we are aware of these days. Christian martyrs do not starve themselves to death in protest, nor do they seek to take as many with them in acts of war or terrorism. Such acts may have a place in war or politics – or they may not – but that is a discussion for another day. The point is that they are not the acts of Christian martyrs.

The take-it-or-leave-it approach essentially signals that there is no more room for manoeuvre. In each of these cases it is the direct conflict between their personal beliefs and the latest ruling from the palace that makes any other position untenable for them. They cannot comply under any circumstances. They have a God whom they worship. On the positive side, they must worship him. On the negative side, they can worship nothing else, no-one else.

There are places in the world where martyrdom is a real issue for our Christian brothers and sisters. However, I suspect that for most of those likely to read this, the issue is not yet whether they are prepared to die for their faith. The take-it-or-leave-it scenario usually comes with a lower price tag. Perhaps it is promotion, or the promotion after that. Maybe it is our job.

Nonetheless, the take-it-or-leave-it approach, with no room for manoeuvre, is probably a position that we do not need to reach quite as often as we do. Despite the volatile times in which he lives, we are only aware that Daniel encounters it once in a lifetime. Of course, under the wrong circumstances, once in a lifetime is significant. In my working career, I have only reached one interview where I thought my principles might cost me my job. Having said that, I can look back on many occasions where I have raised the stakes too quickly, and lost the contract, the friendship, the working relationship in consequence.

And what happens when we finally reach that position? In the cases of Daniel and his friends, they are remarkably and miraculously delivered. In my interview, the management backed me instead of sacking me and I was greatly relieved. I had probably been a pessimist over the worst-case scenario, anyway.

So what should our attitude be to this take-it-or-leave-it mode of negotiation? Even from Daniel, I would have thought we should regard it as an extreme form of negotiation and seek to avoid it where possible. However, where it is necessary, it is a valid approach and can lead to spectacular results – which we shall consider later when exploring the way in which God is at work in the palace.

Tiered negotiations

We first become aware of Daniel's skill in this area when he discovers that, having made the grade for his apprenticeship at the palace, the diet is unacceptable. So why did he decide to go vegetarian? Presumably it was not due to any convictions about meat itself, since certain fish, animals, insects and birds were allowed under the Jewish regulations (Lev 11) and it appears that Daniel was eating meat again later on in his life (Dan 10:2,3). It may have been that later on Daniel had some control over the preparation of his food, but that at this stage he did not want to run the risk of eating proscribed animals. Perhaps he wanted to avoid the risk of eating fat or blood, also proscribed (Lev 3:17), or of consuming meat that had been in some way inappropriately prepared (e.g. Exod 23:19). Perhaps, in view of the fact that he is determined to avoid certain foods and drink, he is like St Paul's friends in Corinth and was concerned about the rituals to which the king's meals might have been subject (1 Cor 8:1-12).

Whatever the reason, Daniel finds himself facing a matter of conscience. At first sight, this appears to be a take-it-or-leave-it situation. However, before he reaches an impasse with the management, he tries to negotiate. Presumably he does not have that much time, since he must eat daily. On the other hand, the wording indicates that Daniel found time to think the matter through – 'But Daniel resolved not to defile himself with the royal food and wine' (Dan 1:8).

Daniel actually allows himself two attempts to salvage the situation before he is forced to make a last-ditch take-it-or-leave-it stand. First, he approaches the chief official (Dan 1:8). Although this manager does not go along with Daniel, we read that God made Daniel a favourite of this man. Perhaps this chap gives Daniel some ideas for the second half of his plan. However, the first step has enabled Daniel to test the water in several ways. He knows, for instance, that the chief official is well disposed towards him. If it were left to the chief official, Daniel knows that he would not have a problem. However, he also knows the chief official's problem, which is that his neck is on the line if Daniel and his friends are seen to fall short of the healthy condition in which they were entrusted to him. Most of us would be so concerned with our own bind that we would probably class the chief official's problem as decidedly minor. Daniel, however, understands and gives full weight to the chief official's position.

Daniel's second negotiation is lower down the chain, with the guard (Dan 1:11-14). I'm not sure how you read the passage, but it appears to me that Daniel offers a meal swap to the guard. Daniel also knows now that the only thing likely to embarrass the chief official would be the ill health of himself or his colleagues. Given this, he makes a bargain to safeguard the guard's position in the eyes of his management ('test your servants... then compare'). Presumably the guard and his friends, colleagues or family, are only too pleased to upgrade their meal ticket, while providing Daniel with cheaper vegetables and water. Whether the chief official turns a blind eye to this arrangement or remains unaware of it is not clear to me. However, the excellent health of this group of exiles ensures that the issue never surfaces again.

Daniel's approach here is an amalgam of faith and action. He needs God's help to grant him favour with the chief official (and presumably plays his part in keeping the relationship open and responsive). He trusts God to ensure that the more basic diet does not plunge him into illness. We see a similar pattern in Esther's experience, where again, she wins the favour of Hegai who has charge of the harem and does all he can to enhance her chances of success (Esth 2:8,9).

So Daniel listens carefully to the chief official's reasoning and, presumably, manages to leave himself space to negotiate with the guard. The chief official does not appear to veto Daniel's diet, explaining instead that he cannot afford to be caught.

Finally, Daniel manages the interesting challenge of not undermining any of the management layers above him. He achieves this by the remarkable step of de-escalating the issue. Most of us would have done things the other way around. We would have tried the guard first and, if that failed, we would have appealed to his boss. This would have left the guard in a tricky position, since even if the higher appeal had been successful, his relationship with Daniel would still have been trashed – and it is the guard with whom Daniel must deal daily. Had the higher appeal failed there would have been considerable ill will about the place to complicate the take-it-or-leave-it phase of the negotiation. I am not saying that de-escalating the negotiation is the way to do it, but it works here, and it is a very smooth piece of work.

This management of the situation indicates to me something of Daniel's mastery of negotiation and relationships. He manages to pitch each appeal at the right level and to minimise the downside risks at the same time. I remember talking to a hospital consultant a couple of years ago. He was explaining the way he and his colleagues felt compelled to negotiate with the management in their hospital. Basically, they told their management that they could not be responsible for patient safety, if the measures they were proposing were not implemented. If they failed to convince that layer of management, they would continue to escalate the problem on up – until it was outside the hospital, if necessary.

Now I understand something of the problems in hospital management systems – today's paper claims that the NHS has more managers than beds! I can see why clinicians often feel they can only adopt a take-it-or-leave-it stance, and must escalate the problem upwards. At times, there may seem to be no other negotiating foothold. However, Daniel has little room for negotiation and yet emerges with a successful result and his working relationships intact. The difficulty with escalation is that the relationships at ground level become increasingly awkward. Also, the higher the problem goes, the less influence you have over the solution. By the time it has been politicised, spun several ways by successive layers of evaluators and raked over by the media, who knows what the outcome will be? And by the time it has bounced that high, you will have to live with the decision, however unreasonable or unpalatable it has become.

So a combination of natural ability, skilful negotiation and faith in God to manage the rest, leads to a very satisfactory outcome. Although he is still young – perhaps still a teenager – he finds a strategy that diffuses the risk over more than one encounter and engages more than one player. Like finessing in bridge, you may be able to play your cards so that you can afford to lose one or two tricks before you reach the make or break play.

You have only to look around your workplace, your neighbourhood, your church, your school, to realise that most people are blissfully unaware of such strategies. All too quickly we reach an impasse. If it goes our way, we hustle on to the next impasse. If it fails, we have boxed ourselves into a corner from which it may take us some time to free ourselves.

Creating time

Any negotiator will tell you that fortune favours those with time on their side. At work I went through a phase when I spent some time looking at negotiation. One of the stories floating about at the time concerned an American and a Japanese team setting out to win a major construction contract. Both teams leased local housing and office space. However, as the negotiations dragged on, the US team found it had to renew the three-month contract on its premises. Later, it came out that the Japanese had taken out a three-year lease from the start.

In our day of instant decisions this is an important lesson to remember. In the episode of the king's dream (Dan 2), there appears to be no time at all. His junior position in the hierarchy means that Daniel has not been party to the negotiations between the king on the one hand, and his magicians, astrologers and wise men on the other. In view of the king's demand that they tell him his dream before they interpret it for him, it is not too surprising that it all quickly reaches the last-ditch phase and the king opts to ditch the lot.

Daniel first becomes aware of his predicament when the executioners arrive with the warrant. We read that Daniel addresses Arioch, commander of the king's guard, 'with wisdom and tact' (Dan 2:14) – perhaps the understatement of the book. Rather than complaining that the decree is unreasonable, Daniel uses the argument that it seems precipitate, harsh even, and he buys time. He is admitted to the king and gains the time to find out about the dream.

Now what sort of person commands that kind of respect from his executioners? A rather unusual person, to be sure. A modern example might be Nelson Mandela, who by all accounts, conducted himself with dignity throughout his imprisonment and emerged to become a mature statesman in difficult times. But your life is probably full of people who manage to take the heat out of situations, who do not waste energy railing against the stupidities and inconsistencies of the management but focus on getting the job done under the most trying of circumstances. I can really only admire from afar on this one. In Daniel's shoes, I am sure I would have been consumed with frustration and anger at the sheer injustice of it all. I am sure I would have wasted the scant time at my disposal in useless argument and fatal ranting.

And how easy it would have been to focus on that fruitless argument about whether the king was being fair. To be fair to the king, he probably felt he had been duped by his wise men before. They probably would come up with some story, given the basics of his dream. And so he does not even give them the basics of his dream. But none of this makes his behaviour any fairer to those he commands. Daniel avoids this line, presumably not because it is flawed, but because it will not work in these circumstances. There will be times ahead for that but first one has to survive.

One-to-one

A final aspect of Daniel's approach is that he tries, as far as we can tell, to deal with individuals. He speaks personally to the chief official and then to the guard. There were other options. He might have organised mass action. He might have found a way to foment dissent amongst other ethnic groups for whom, too, the king's table contained an element of offence. Today he might have had the options of circulating a memo outlining his grievance, or of winging out an e-mail, copied to all and sundry.

Starting one-to-one is certainly the biblical way, especially within a fellowship: 'If your brother sins against you, go and show him his fault, just between the two of you. If he listens to you, you have won your brother over. But if he will not listen, take one or two others along, so that "every matter may be established by the testimony of two or three witnesses." If he refuses to listen to them, tell it to the church; and if he refuses to listen even to the church, treat him as you would a pagan or a tax collector' (Matt 18:15-17). If you are worried that this looks like escalation, remember that de-escalation is a bit of a bonus. Furthermore, this example is in the context of the church, where conflict is being managed against a common moral framework.

I had a boss, once, who really helped me with this one. Perhaps someone had splattered me or my team with mud, as part of who knows what turf war. Perhaps a whole tranche of funding had just been stitched together with several stakeholders when someone influential would suggest that it ought to go through a top-level review in six months. I cannot remember all the causes, but I would often sit down and write a spectacular letter or e-mail. A voice in the back of my head would suggest that I ought to get cover from my boss and he would come back to me. He would tell me it was a wonderful e-mail and that its purpose was now done in allowing me to vent my fury. Delete the e-mail, ditch the draft memo, sleep on it and ring the person in the morning. Better still, see if you could make an appointment and see them in person. He lived by this creed himself and showed by example that he could unravel the most intricate problems involving difficult people by patiently visiting them one by one.

He taught me that you only write things down to confirm agreements – real agreements. I have also found that you can write things down to congratulate people, without 'phoning first. But as a guide, take the personal approach, secure the agreement. Go into print afterwards if necessary. What does Jesus say? 'As you are going with your adversary to the magistrate, try hard to be reconciled to him on the way, or he may drag you off to the judge, and the judge turn you over to the officer, and the officer throw you into prison. I tell you, you will not get out until you have paid the last penny' (Luke 12:58,59). Keep the dialogue going.

As someone who has been too free with his e-mails in the past, I have to say that Christians need to be careful what goes into their e-mails. Moving from a controlled, industrial environment to the much less regulated academic sphere, I was amazed at what people will throw at each other in e-mails. Cadences that are alive to the heat of the moment can look leaden, hollow or out of all proportion a day or so later. A friend who works in health is regulated by the rule that you cannot respond within 24 hours to emotive e-mails.

From the receiving end, angry e-mails are not that fun, either. I received a wild missive from a Christian friend a while back. I had done something a bit stupid, but there was a method to the madness, and he had not fully understood all I was trying to do. My old instinct would have been to rebut some of the content and to justify what I had done. In the end, I just e-mailed back suggesting we talk about it. I think I went a little further in saying that I couldn't understand why he had written in the way he had – and that, too, was stupid of me. The talk didn't really settle things, but at least the matter subsided more quickly than it might otherwise have done.

The spoken word, in context, with its ability to respond to the evolving negotiation is certainly the best approach. John Pollock has introduced me to many great Christians through his biographies. In telling George Whitefield's story he shows how the written word is such a poor tool in negotiation as Whitefield and John Wesley burst into print in a major theological bust-up. If I remember rightly, no less an atheist than Benjamin Franklin advised Whitefield against publishing!

So a third key to Daniel's success in negotiating appears to be the personal dialogue.

What are the lessons for us?

Before we try to turn this into lessons for us, I think it is fun just to pause and watch a skilful practitioner at work. If Daniel's life were a game of football and these were examples of the goals he scored, there would be action replays, during the game, after the game, at the end of the month. These would have been in contention for goal of the year. If you are like me, you will look back and think of those times in your career when you would have scored had Daniel been your coach. And there is nothing wrong in appreciating excellence, wherever you find it. I do not believe the Bible was ever meant to be a management manual, but to achieve the things they did, the characters had to be exceptional people, and the writers were wonderfully observant to pick up the nuances. Daniel was exceptional – enjoy the show!

And when the main options for Christians at work seem to be all-out opposition or total compliance, Daniel is a refreshing example of someone who was always thinking, always creating room for manoeuvre, always buying time, always one step ahead of the game. And yet he is not devious. His ingenuity is exercised in pursuit of a clear conscience and service to God. Part of being an effective Christian is to be good at what you do. Daniel gives us some clues about being good in a decidedly difficult environment. And this reflection will be all the more fun if you have failed in the same arena.

There is no easier way to switch on the light than to see someone doing it right when you have done it wrong. Back to that learning spell on negotiation that I was talking about earlier: part of the experience was to listen to a set of tapes on negotiation. My main need to negotiate was to sell research services. Sometimes it was to fund my team, sometimes for a wider group across the organisation. I don't suppose you will need to think about it for long to realise that selling research is a bit of a loser's game. When can I have it? Well we'll have some results in three years... prototypes a year later – but cheer up, the patents will be good for ages! What will it cost me? Well this first phase comes to... An Italian director (great negotiator) once asked me whether he would be better off putting ten thousand pounds into my project, or blowing it on a holiday in the Maldives. I could sense a strong case for the Maldives. As I listened to the tapes, however, I realised that most of the barriers I had encountered were standard moves. There were answers! Been there, had it done to me, I thought, and then listened hard for the counters.

I particularly remembered one move that people used against us time and again. The chap on the tape explained it in a car sales scenario. Someone has just inherited from Aunt Meg and wants to buy a new car. The salesperson is already counting the bonus on the car when there is some bad news. Sadly, the car is eighteen thousand pounds and Auntie has only left fifteen thousand pounds. How can the salesperson go crackers at this heir for wasting time or trying to drag the price down? It's all Auntie Meg's fault with her inconsiderate provision – and she is not even around to sort out the mess she has created! How many times have I thought I was there, only to be told that the R&D budget had been cut, was under review, or had been channelled into critical research in support of some unforeseen emergency! But the author taught me that there are ways to deal with such tactics without exhuming Auntie Meg or walking away in disgust. Just knowing that there were answers was a great encouragement.

And I hope Daniel fulfils something of that role for you when you find work a bit much. If you always feel under pressure; have too little time; are never high enough up the food chain; or are always wanting to stop the merry-go-round to catch your breath, Daniel was there. He succeeded. By God's grace, you can, too.

The other reason why Daniel's management of conflict is important is that our Christian lives are so often scarred with conflict. It seems that a major bust-up in the first term is par for the course in full-time Christian service. The reasons will differ, but if you were a bookie or an insurance agent, you would have little compunction in shortening the odds or raising the premiums against collateral damage. My prejudice here is that sending organisations, including missions, must take a large share of the blame. I believe the informality of the roles to which people are called leads to sloppiness in structures, lack of accountability and a failure to face key issues and deal with them openly.

But part of the problem is also that those in training for Christian service are not really taught the lessons of Daniel. There are times when no-one is more unreasonable than a colleague who is driven by a vision. The environments Christian workers inhabit are often shot through with unusual stresses, not least the tensions of closely knit teams. In addition, there may be an unfamiliar culture or language, perhaps poverty in an all too familiar culture. Maybe the lack of a formal framework – that is provided for most of us by our 'day job' – can create motivational problems and a sense of lethargy. Christian workers need a good set of tools for conflict resolution. They need to understand which approaches work best with their own personality, which methods are best suited to which situations and how to mix and match them as new issues emerge, mature and are finally resolved. Daniel and Nehemiah are great characters to study if you are into conflict resolution. If I were training full-time workers, we would spend about 20% of our time looking at the down-to-earth lessons on conflict management.

Our churches, of course, were designed to show the love and unity of God: 'A new command I give you: Love one another. As I have loved you, so you must love one another. By this all men will know that you are my disciples, if you love one another' (John 13:34,35). And I am as guilty of flouting this command as the next person, perhaps more so. The really good news is that there are ways to deal with conflict. There will always be deep disagreements between Christians. If Jesus really is worth more than everything else in our lives, if he really is worth following in the fanatical way that those who first knew him understood him to demand, then we will hold our views about that calling very dear. We are likely to have strong feelings in all issues associated with our worship. I was discussing hymns with a friend who confided to me somewhat mischievously that he was quite certain that some of those in his church with very strong views on hymns were tone deaf. And, on reflection, why not? There are those who choose hymns because of the words and those who choose on the tunes, and those who balance these tastes with other considerations, also. Certainly, if we were to avoid all hymns with dodgy words or musical sequences, there would not be much to sing about.

Once issues are important, they are worth fighting about. How much should vicars, ministers or pastors be paid? One family's quiet conservatism is another's abject poverty. One group's attempt to set a salary around the church's mean income, will provide a standard of living beyond the reach of others within the same church. Debate, by all means, but by what methods? Should we use real wine in a common cup at communion (which preserves some of the original imagery, but carries hygienic risks and may, if you use an alcoholic wine, provide a potential problem for reformed alcoholics) or go for the tiny glasses (which require much more effort and demolish part of the imagery, but allow each glass to be filled with juice or cordial rather than wine)? Whichever side you are on, it is not hard to cast the opposition unsympathetically. I went to a church where we came up with a wonderful compromise and used different approaches on different Sundays!

Daniel tells us a lot about dealing with emotive issues and matters of conscience, in a way that preserves the relationships. In my view the church business meeting is a difficult arena for resolving such conflicts unless a great deal of preparation has been done. But I have seen highly emotive decisions reached when the leadership has been able to take a lead, circulate consultatory information, gather views widely, and slow the pace, so that people do not feel they are being rushed into things.

Management

On several occasions in the story, Daniel and his companions are promoted in their secular jobs. Again, this is new territory, away from the more usual Old Testament roles of priest, prophet, king, farmer, shepherd or general. After interpreting the king's dream, the king appoints him to a senior position at the palace in charge of all the wise men, while his influence is sufficient to ensure positions in the provincial administration for his friends (Dan 2:48,49). Later on, his friends discover that their encounter with the furnace provides strong grounds for promotion in the system (Dan 3:30).

As I understand it, when Nebuchadnezzar eventually died, Babylon descended into chaos following this extended period of stability, and a series of monarchs emerged. Daniel survives this disastrous period, although his career appears to fade, perhaps on several occasions, and he is an unknown by Belshazzar's time (Dan 5:10-12), although he is again promoted, very briefly (and perhaps hazardously) in the dying hours of Belshazzar's reign (Dan 5:29). Darius recognises Daniel's potential and he prospers in office once more (Dan 6:2,3). Throughout all this, Daniel realises that his star will not always grow brighter, and that there will be times in which others will take his place before the king.

Clearly, I am a Daniel fan. I read Daniel as an excellent example of someone who walks close to God and pursues a secular career. You could read the book more cynically and see him as a manipulator who gets it in the neck once in a while and fades once he has ceased to be flavour of the month. My unease with such an approach lies in reconciling it with Daniel's evident integrity and the way in which he enjoys such an open relationship with God. There are, of course, plenty of honest people who are still a pain to work with. However, what little evidence we have, combined with the implications of his close relationship with God, and the favour he enjoys over a very long period of time and under more than one dynasty leads me to assume he was actually rather good at what he did.

And at the end of the day, Daniel cuts the mustard at the palace because he is good at what he does. The exiles had no other foothold in the palace. Their end of term report is exceptional (Dan 1:19,20). Daniel's first promotion is on the basis of merit. The story indicates that the rest were on exactly the same basis – 'Now Daniel so distinguished himself among the administrators and the satraps by his exceptional qualities that the king planned to set him over the whole kingdom' (Dan 6:3).

Nehemiah is another exile who was really good at what he did. I do not know whether his position as cup-bearer involved training to hone his talents, or whether operating in such circles just exposed him to the best project management of the day so that his natural skill in the area enabled him to pick up the lessons quickly. However, everything he does marks him out as an accomplished project manager. He plans and prays before he speaks out (Neh 1), he reconnoitres before he finalises and shares his plans (Neh 2:11,12). He quantifies tasks and can set time scales with the king (Neh 2:6). He is at ease with the paperwork and tools of office, requesting documents for safe conduct and resources (Neh 2:7-9) and is happy to accept the King's protection. (Note how Ezra, another Jewish exile and a priest, is uneasy at appealing for any protection other than that of God alone (Ezra 8:22).) Nehemiah gets the job done at all costs and is much more confrontational with people (e.g. Neh 13:25) than Daniel would dream of being.

There is a simple message here for us. Approval before God is difficult if there is no approval before people. Remember Luke's summary of those years of missing narrative in Jesus' own life? 'And Jesus grew in wisdom and stature, and in favour with God and men' (Luke 2:52). Paul's approach to secular masters follows the same lines: 'Obey them not only to win their favour when their eye is on you, but like slaves of Christ, doing the will of God from your heart. Serve wholeheartedly, as if you were serving the Lord, not men, because you know that the Lord will reward everyone for whatever good he does, whether he is slave or free' (Eph 6:6-8). Paul's qualifications for church leaders, carries the rider: 'He must also have a good reputation with outsiders' (1 Tim 3:7). Add in Paul's surprising and very direct warnings about laziness (2 Thess 3:11,12; 1 Tim 5:13; Tit 1:12-14) and the Bible provides us with a practical patchwork of advice about our approach to work. A complete look at the topic would also consider the opposite extreme, of Christians who are so taken up with success at work that all else takes second place. But the key message here is that being good at what you do is important. It is worth praying for if you are struggling. Good workmanship is worth it.

Boundary lines

The other interesting facet of Daniel's career is that he ends up being managed by and in turn managing people whose moral outlooks diametrical oppose his own. It appears that, following the interpretation of Nebuchadnezzar's first dream, Daniel was put in charge of the entire cohort of magicians, enchanters, sorcerers and astrologers (Dan 2:48). What a predicament! His manager is a despot and Daniel must have seen many harsh, cruel and immoral things done by the king. His workforce is devoted to magical arts that were completely out of bounds to the devout Jew. And yet there is no evidence that Daniel finds a need to extricate himself from his working environment.

There are some questions at the end to try and explore further the issues that this raises, but I think there are a couple of ways in which Daniel's example is helpful today. After all, just as Daniel shares a joint citizenship as a Babylonian and a Jew, so Paul asserts that Christians, too, have this bridging role between two nationalities: 'So from now on we regard no one from a worldly point of view… Therefore, if anyone is in Christ, he is a new creation; the old has gone, the new has come! All this is from God, who reconciled us to himself through Christ and gave us the ministry of reconciliation: that God was reconciling the world to himself in Christ, not counting men's sins against them. And he has committed to us the message of reconciliation. We are therefore Christ's ambassadors, as though God were making his appeal through us' (2 Cor 5:16-20). And an ambassador lives and works locally, but has allegiances that may lie thousands of miles away.

So, if we try to take Daniel's lead, how does this help us? First, it seems to me that it sets some sort of limit on the role of personal conscience. Daniel clearly believes he can serve in this pagan court and be loyal to the king, despite that fact that those around him would have been behaving in ways that he would have found immoral, perhaps even offensive. Furthermore, when Daniel realises the punishment God plans to bring on Nebuchadnezzar, he is appalled (Dan 4:19)! And yet it is because Daniel is part of this scene that he is able to break such awful news to Nebuchadnezzar. Perhaps Daniel is one of the people responsible for holding the kingdom together during Nebuchadnezzar's spell of insanity. Because he is there, Daniel plays a part in God's plan to face Nebuchadnezzar up with his pride – and perhaps also to be part of the solution. He could not have played that role in absentia.

The story of Esther takes a similar line. I find some of the characters in Esther much harder to read than those in Daniel. For instance, is Mordecai a pushy uncle determined to cash in on his niece's beauty? Is he a bit cranky, creating unnecessary problems for himself and his people through his unwillingness to compromise at any level? Or is he a straightforward character, so loyal to his adoptive homeland that he will happily finger the putative assassins, Bigthana and Teresh (Esth 2:21-23) when they plan to kill the king? However we read it, Esther is prepared to go to the palace and become queen in Vashti's place. Of course, the pay-off here is that Esther is strategically placed to help her own people in desperate times.

So is this a licence to bury our heads in the sand, ignoring all the moral dilemmas at work except those that specifically affect us in our jobs? Clearly not. In charging his followers with the task of being salt and light (Matt 5:13-16), Jesus expects them to bring a tang of holiness and joy to their environment. A Christian friend was telling me recently about the only time his boss had asked him to do something he felt went too far. He explained to his boss why he felt uncomfortable with it and in the end, the boss himself felt sufficiently uncomfortable to take a different approach. And that is how it should be. Often, one person putting forward a clear position clarifies the issue in the minds of others and, in a small way, the company changes for the better.

But I think Daniel's example indicates that there are limits as to how far we need to take this. In days when large corporations involve wealth and power on a scale that even Nebuchadnezzar might have envied and would certainly have appreciated, how much of the corporate morality should an individual Christian feel responsible for? If your local hi-tech company is taken over by an international conglomerate that is exploiting its workforce in another country and engaged in dodgy business practice somewhere else in the world, are you compelled to resign in protest? To me Daniel says, not necessarily.

Second, I think Daniel helps us to draw a line between professional and personal relationships. It is hard, for instance, to see how Daniel could have shared much common moral ground with the sorcerers in his team. And yet he was in charge of them. A situation such as this should never have arisen within the old environment before the exile and if it had, the result would have been a life-or-death struggle between Daniel and his team. As a comparative example, you might consider Elijah's treatment of the prophets of Baal (1 Kings 18:40). In fact, if the link between Haman the Agagite (Esth 3:1) and King Agag (1 Sam 15:8-33) be proven, we might even have an example of just such a life-or-death struggle in the book of Esther. Agag, king of the Amalekites, against whom the Israelites had waged war since the time of Moses (Exod 17:8-16), was put to death by Samuel, in the reign of Saul, son of Kish from the tribe of Benjamin. Mordecai's lineage (Esth 2:5) shows him to be a descendant of (the same?) Kish (I'm sorry, but I am unable to work in a line about Kish and kin). Perhaps, 500 years after the encounter with Saul, this racial and religious backdrop creates a deadly environment for some of the Jews, even though both parties are now being integrated into a new society.

Getting back to Daniel, however, we can see that he does not feel compelled to stamp his moral position on those around him. Clearly his relationship with God and the moral position that flows from it is non-negotiable. However, he will find himself working with people whose beliefs are strongly opposed to his own – and he is able to work with them.

While the exiles are able to work in such an environment, it is not, as we have already noted, without its dangers and underlying tensions surface occasionally. It is the astrologers who shop Shadrach, Meshach and Abednego to the king when they fail to worship the image (Dan 3:8). It is less clear that there is a moral or ethical motivation when the administrators and satraps seek to undermine Daniel's position in government (Dan 6:1-5). Envy seems to be the driving force, although they soon recognise that his unusual set of beliefs offer them a special opportunity to plot his downfall. And I guess that will happen once in a while. Once in a while, someone will take a moral stand and it will not be forgotten. Sometimes your colleagues will find that it would be easier to operate without you and, when an opportunity presents itself, they may well make the most of it.

The message of Daniel seems to be that we should trust God should something like this ever happen, but should not worry about the potential for such an event ahead of time. And Peter reminds us that we should be sure it is really our faith that is the cause of the antagonism: 'If you are insulted because of the name of Christ, you are blessed, for the Spirit of glory and of God rests on you. If you suffer, it should not be as a murderer or thief or any other kind of criminal, or even as a meddler. However, if you suffer as a Christian, do not be ashamed, but praise God that you bear that name' (1 Pet 4:14-16).

For most people, this is an encouragement to manage and to try to be managed in an open and confident way, seeking to establish strong working relationships with peers and management alike. However, where we have jobs that involve a special ethical or moral dimension, I believe Daniel sheds important light on how to operate with those whose ethics may be different from, or even hostile to, our own.

In moving away from the sheltered environment of Judah and succeeding in senior secular roles, I believe Daniel, his friends, and exiles such as Nehemiah are pioneers. Instead of barricading themselves into an ethnic or religious ghetto, they have the confidence and integrity to engage with and succeed in a variety of morally difficult scenarios. What wonderful examples!

Thinking it through

1. You have an idea for developing a new and highly profitable service for your company to sell. The Finance Director has taken a shine to you and will, you are sure, like the idea if you can pitch it at that level. However, your own boss has told you to focus on a remedial plan for a product that no-one has been able to patch up for the past 18 months – and you are not confident of your chances. The company needs something to go right quickly. What are your options? What are the risks? How is your Christianity likely to be perceived in each case?

2. You have fought to get a pay rise for one of your team members against a management that has resolutely refused one. However, when this person got a better job offer, the general manager instantly comes up with a pay rise of twice the level you were trying for. How do you handle the next team meeting where salary is back at the top of the agenda? As a Christian where do your loyalties lie?

3. You are having trouble getting a new piece of equipment through its trials when one of the directors phones to inform you that the release documentation is needed urgently. When you explain the technical problems, he tells you not to burden him with details – he just needs the signed certificates by Friday. In the heat of the moment, you ask him to put his request in writing and he tells you not to be so stupid. How do you take it from there?

4. As a field engineer you have heard rumours that the latest chief accountant has some unusual business practices. Should you take any action and, if so, what?

5. As an employee of a start-up company, you are delighted to discover that you are about to be acquired. Although your company's operations will remain unchanged, the purchaser also owns a small business that sells distinctly dodgy products to a number of unsavoury regimes. If the sale goes through, your share options will clear your mortgage. How would you decide whether or not you have a problem?

6. List the five jobs you think were most likely to have caused Christians ethical problems in the '60s. How might such a list look today? How about in 40 years from now?

7. What trends in the secular working environment represent the greatest opportunities to Christians and which are likely to prove most difficult?

8. You arrive home on the evening before a fortnight's holiday and pick-up a frosty message from a friend at church. You realise that an issue that has smouldered for months has been sparked into a crisis and you are quite sure you have been badly misquoted at some stage. What are the main issues for you and your friend likely to be? How would you plan to proceed?

9. The young people have been discussing the teaching provided at the morning service and would like to stimulate a discussion on its effectiveness. Since there is a church business meeting coming up, they suggest raising it as an AOB. What other options do you think they might have and what are the risks associated with each? In the end, they raise the matter at the business meeting. What do you think was the outcome?

10. A friend of yours has had an idea to twin your church with a church in Mexico. There are a number of Spanish speakers in your fellowship and there are projects in Mexico that would enable your young people develop in their faith and help this struggling potential partner. However, the pastor has always been opposed to it, principally because it is likely to be a huge distraction without any clear prospect of long-term benefit. The

relationship between your friend and the pastor has deteriorated over the past three months, and most of the church has been corralled into one or the other's camp. You are asked at short notice to take the chair at the church business meeting in ten days and note this issue on the agenda. What steps might you take to aid the debate and defuse the tension?

11. In what ways are Nehemiah and Daniel alike? In what ways are they different? What particular qualities and skills made each successful in his sphere?

12. To what extent do Daniel and Esther find similar ways to prosper at court? What is Esther's main characteristic as an exemplar for young executives?

3

The long haul

So what happens to Daniel's career? I used to feel that engineering had a special way of turning bright young things into grand old men without any genuine period of greatness in between. So many careers that caught the wave early were beached before they had gathered much momentum. One of the sad things about the recent stock market collapse and scandals that have shaken the US scene in particular is the train of relatively young managers who may never work again.

So, even if he can hack the pace, how much further can Daniel go?

A straightforward (and very conservative) reading of the record would have Daniel being deported to Babylon in, say 605 BC and still receiving revelations in Cyrus' third year (Dan 10:1 – 537 BC), around seventy years later. If he is a teenager at the start, he is nearing ninety by chapter 10. Clearly, the whole business of dating Daniel's life is highly contentious. I have explained some of my reasons for adopting the perspective I have – and you may decide that a better chronology fits the facts. Whatever the details, if you accept a Daniel rooted in history at all, he seems to have been around for a very long time.

On this reckoning, Daniel's first career starts in his late teens or early twenties and lasts, perhaps, until Nebuchadnezzar's death in 562 BC, when Daniel might be nearing 60. As we have noted, Nebuchadnezzar left a power vacuum behind, and the next couple of decades were not good years for the empire. Daniel appears to have been passed over in these subsequent administrations, seeing a very brief and spectacular promotion in the dying hours before the fall of Babylon (539 BC) when he would have been, as we have observed, well into his eighties. Subsequently, his influence waxes again.

As he approached 50, it must have seemed that his career was over. My guess is that he would not have seen his career as an entity in its own right, in the way we might do. I have no idea what the retirement arrangements would have been, but in rising to such heights, Daniel would presumably have amassed sufficient personal wealth to enable him to take a relaxed view of the future.

The big problem with having to take a back seat, of course, is the pain of losing power. I remember stepping from a line management position into a business development role. I found it painful to see decisions being taken by others about teams I had helped to build. Perhaps Daniel sensed the same loss. And in any career, there will be reverses. But there may also be changes in role that do not necessarily equate to promotion or demotion in a conventional sense.

Certainly, it is not all bad news for the Jews after Daniel loses influence following Nebuchadnezzar's death. Nebuchadnezzar's successor releases the old king, Jehoiachin, from prison and treats him with kindness and respect, promoting him above the other captured monarchs in Babylon (2 Kings 25:27-30).

Although Daniel is a very old man before we see him again in court, reading the writing on the wall (Dan 5:13-31) at the end of Belshazzar's reign, he is not idle. However, a different sort of ministry opens up for him and we find him having his first vision in the first year of Belshazzar's reign, perhaps 551/552 BC. This is tricky territory for a non-specialist such as me, but I understand that Belshazzar is acting king in the absence of his father, Nabonidus, who came to the throne in 556 BC and does not appear in the biblical record. This is half a century after Daniel first arrived in Babylon, and as we have said, he must be around seventy. The dreams and visions furnish much of the material in the second half of the book. Later still, Daniel is moved as a very old man into yet another ministry – that of prayer for his people (Dan 9:4-19).

From a career perspective, there are several observations that may be helpful. First, careers wax and wane. Early success is no guarantee of later acceptance. Careers may well have lean patches. As I write, the over-50s are being thrown onto the scrap heap and appear to have little chance of significant follow-on careers, but that may all change as the economy cycles on and demand for workers rises once again. Had Daniel worked at the turn of this millennium, he would have been finished after his first career under Nebuchadnezzar. And it may have looked that way to Daniel at the time.

The important thing is that other ministries open up. Alongside his political and administrative career, with its lengthy lean patches, Daniel develops other roles. These would probably not have been valued by his peers at court, but his visions and prayer have stood the test of time. I wonder how you would have felt at the peak of an international career to be offered a new role in visions and prayer. For most of us, this would have looked like a kick in the teeth. And yet, the text gives as much emphasis to Daniel's later life as to his earlier exploits. The mysteries have certainly scored over the histories with the theologians down the centuries.

And we live in the serial-career era! Many of my work colleagues retired well before 65 and for a while it looked like few would have to work beyond 55. At the same time we are staying healthier for longer. I read somewhere that the decades from 50 to 70 are providing an unexpected golden era for many with the resources and opportunities for a rewarding life, free from the stresses of raising a family and before the prospect of a more restricted lifestyle materialises.

Some choose to keep on working, perhaps not as avidly as before, but working none the less. A taxi-driver who would occasionally drive me home from the rank at the station, was 83. I asked him why he still went out to work and he said that his friends who had stopped working were dead. I was chatting to someone after church last Sunday who had completed a career in the forces and was halfway through retraining for a second career. A friend of mine wound up a building business he had successfully built from scratch, to direct a Christian charity. Many of us can expect to be active well into our seventies or even eighties. The possibility that we may have several quite different careers is increasingly realistic, too.

It seems to me that there are at least two ways in which we can apply this to our spiritual journey. The first is to focus on developing new ministries in our churches and fellowships as the heat eases at work. At a time when we might otherwise worry about loss of prestige or influence at work, or when we find our careers are shunting into a siding, there is the opportunity to refocus on a different sphere of our lives. The second is to take the early retirement package and get involved in a much more dedicated capacity with something new.

Provided we can offer our services to God in a selfless manner and find, with others, the gifts with which we can make our contribution and impact, the former has the potential to enrich our fellowships immeasurably. So many of the difficult tasks in our churches are better done by those with considerable experience of life. While there are roles that consume vast amounts of energy, there are many that require a steady hand instead. So many pastoral problems need a wise listener. So many of our committees need people who can take the long view. So much of our teaching needs really practical application. So many of our financial decisions would be better made by those with significant experience of managing money. It is not necessarily the high profile, high impact contribution that is most helpful, but the steady, thoughtful, spiritual application of truths gleaned over a lifetime of walking with God that brings the greater benefit.

I sometimes wonder whether Daniel thought this vision stuff was second best. If this new phase only became viable because of a lull in his normal career, was it really worth it? From a personal viewpoint, I started writing during a time when I did not feel my career was going anywhere. In a sense, the writing was a release to begin with, and yet it has brought a balance to my life and been a lot of fun, too.

We will try to explore how this new ministry related to his personality, training and gifts when we come to think about the visions – but what did this new ministry feel like? Did it take time before there really was a vision worth writing down? Was it something he had to develop? There are no real clues, although there is evidence that he found the whole process extremely draining (Dan 7:28; 8:27; 10:17). Was he worried that he was going mad, and that these new experiences were simply delusory? I have no idea and yet the fact remains that Daniel, as a character in Bible history, is known by millions more people than could ever have appreciated the impact of his political skills during his lifetime. His sideline initiative has made an enduring contribution to our understanding of God's heart for the world.

And a new ministry may require developing new skills. To exploit your skill in presentations as part of a teaching ministry may require unaccustomed study. It may mean formal study. It is likely to require personal reading. Formalising your experience with people to a point where you can make a pastoral impact will almost certainly require training. You may need to focus on special skills in order to move your contribution from the high profile leader you were in your secular career to the team player you need to be in playing a part in your local church. My builder friend, for instance, is learning new ways of being in charge now that he is the director of a charity rather than the boss of a commercial enterprise. He has already developed his presentational skills, skills that were rarely required in the tendering process but are essential to his new, public-facing role. The last I heard was someone complimenting him on his ministry in church – presumably as a result of being more relaxed in front of a crowd.

Some churches have formal ways of managing this. A colleague spent the last few years of his research career in training as a lay reader in order to play a new role on retirement at his local Anglican church. There are certainly plenty of choices for those looking to develop a counselling ministry. But beyond that, I am not sure our churches have gotten their heads around the 'Daniel transition' from secular to spiritual service in a systematic way.

An attractive option for some is to retire in their fifties with a reasonable degree of financial security. Unless there is ill health, this opens up perhaps two decades of active ministry. I have two sisters who work in Africa, both with Christian organisations. Both have benefited enormously from people who have come out to help, particularly with educational support for the children. One group of people offering this service has been gappers: students taking a year between secondary education and university. The other class has been retired people with the energy and resources to spend several months at a time away from home and in a very different environment. I think this type of service has a lot going for it. It may all evaporate if stock markets fail to recover and we all end up working into our seventies, but while it lasts, Christians ought to make the most of it.

My Dad was a missionary and a challenging local speaker. People would come up to me after the service and say how much they wished they could have been missionaries. Some would even tell me that they had once sensed the call of God upon their lives but had somehow ploughed on with a more conventional life. Looking back, I wonder how many were genuinely called and how many suffered from poor teaching and came to believe that full-time service was God's first call on every Christian's life. However that may be, the window is opening for many Christians to have that chance to fulfil their longing and do something meaningful for God. We recently had two women speak at our church about their ministry with orphans overseas. One of the speakers was eighty. If you can take the money and run, a second career in Christian service looks like a winner to me.

Time for change

But how can we know if it is time to move into something new? Is a sense of failure a trigger to move into something different, or a spur to do better at the day job? I can identify with those who look at the purposelessness of working life – the endless cycles of meaningless change, budget-setting, budget-cutting, reorganising towards a more hierarchical structure, restructuring towards a flatter team – and understand the urge to do something more meaningful. Wouldn't it be nice to study theology all day, to work in a pastoral team, to do something where the benefits were more tangible and more closely linked with people? After the first string of promotions comes to an end and we realise that we are not going to make the board, is there not something to be said for seeking a change?

I have certainly been tempted at times and have watched with a little envy as a few of my friends have taken the plunge and moved into a new ministry. Against the routine of many occupations, Christian service looks appealing to the individual and the individual may look attractive to the church, mission or other society. Most of us need a push and often the push is an unpleasant surprise, perhaps a lost promotion, an unappealing place in the reorganised structure, a sideways move out of line management.

In a sense, failure is the door to success in many walks of life. I have just been looking at Scott Adams' *The Dilbert Future*. In it, he makes the case (albeit with a degree of tongue in cheek) that his success as a cartoonist came out of his 'complete failure' to succeed in the employ of a local phone company. Clearly there are careers where creativity is unlikely to be recognised as an asset and where skills in mocking the management will undermine rather than enhance one's prospects. As a talented humorist, Scott Adams is able to position his failure in a dead end, downbeat job, as some kind of overall failure, and his inter-national success as a cartoonist as something of an accident. Viewed objectively, however, one can only view as a blessing for him the fact that his first career was not a success. Most people would judge his success solely on the strength of his later fame with the little pictures – particularly if they have ever had any-thing to do with the software industry. With creative types and entrepreneurs, a failure to manage in a conventional setting has been the launch pad to success in running their own show.

On the other hand, we know of plenty of people who are always longing to change, who never get around to it and yet never quite find their niche in their chosen career, either, despite several attempts. This can, of course, be disastrous if they end up wrongly in Christian work. My perception is that most Christian organisations are often more charitable in their selec-tion criteria than their secular counterparts and less enthusiastic in managing or even getting rid of unproductive or unsuitable workers.

Surely this is their great strength. After all, God's great joke is to choose, 'the lowly things of this world and the despised things – and the things that are not – to nullify the things that are' (1 Cor 1:28). Indeed, in that passage, Paul has just remind-ed his audience in Corinth that, 'Not many of you were wise by human standards; not many were influential; not many were of noble birth' (1 Cor 1:26). The church is God's way of using insignificant people – especially people who have come to recognise their own insignificance – in order to challenge socie-ty as a whole. In a sense, one of the biggest difficulties faced by the church today is that it has too much influence, too many powerful people, and too little need of God's support. But I digress.

There are plenty of examples of people who did not make their mark in secular society playing a profound and highly beneficial role in church. In my teens I attended a church with lay leadership. The chap who set the pace was a teacher at the junior school just behind the church – and an exceptionally gift-ed classroom teacher according to those of the family who passed through his care. He never made it to head teacher, nor even to deputy. It may have been that his desire to stay in the area and support the local church precluded some promotion opportunities. Perhaps he was too quiet and insufficiently pushy to raise his profile for preferment. Whatever the reasons, he had a dual career as an ordinary teacher and a well recognised church leader in the area. The church was a great blessing to me in terms of the quality of teaching it provided. It managed in many ways to 'punch above its weight', attracting international speakers and spawning high quality musical initiatives. So how would you have evaluated his career?

And yet again, I have come across people in Christian service, whom I am sure would not survive in any other working environment. This raises an important question for us – how do we know if the spiritual role that beckons is really for us?

Factors for change

How about a track record? Daniel has been successful in the past. He knows objectively that his judgement is sound because he has had to learn to exercise it, and because he has exercised it successfully. When helping people to assess their transition into some type of Christian service, how many times do we explore the level of skill and ability latent in the earlier career? 'Do you see a man skilled in his work? He will serve before kings; he will not serve before obscure men' (Prov 22:29). And you can see why that should be. Earlier, I mentioned a friend who ran a successful building company before deciding to run a Christian charity. As I watch the way he makes decisions in his role with the charity, I can see him drawing on years of experience that served him well in another sector. Alongside the financial and managerial skills you would expect of someone who has built a business, he has that indefinable something that means he gets the job done. Things happen. The charity is not becalmed, it is moving forward, reshaping itself, and developing new services.

How about personal conviction – how helpful is that in deciding whether the new course is right? A sense of personal destiny, conviction or vision is a vital ingredient in taking unusual initiatives. It was his belief that enabled Abraham to hold on for years to God's promise of a son, 'being fully persuaded that God had power to do what he had promised' (Rom 4:21). We sometimes see the same commitment and focus paying off in other sectors of life. In his book *Fermat's Last Theorem*, Simon Singh gets around to the story of Andrew Wyles, the academic who shut himself away for years believing he could finally solve a problem that had perplexed generations of mathematicians. Much had been done to creep up on the solution over the centuries since Fermat first scribbled so frustratingly in the margin of his book, but it was Wyles who pulled it all together. Would you trust yourself to devote that much of your life to a problem that no-one else had been able to close? And yet, in his case, the conviction was well founded. He had to rework his proof at one stage, but it was finally validated, and his name is established.

I am just reading David Livingstone's biography with my elder two sons and can see how important sheer determination was. It has been an interesting read and provided a surprising perspective on the motives and achievements of someone whose life I thought I had a handle on. But what impresses me this time is the sheer energy needed to achieve anything – the long treks endured often in extreme ill health; the lengthy separations from his family; the many times he had to start building from scratch – a house, a well, a garden. Whatever one makes of his vision, it is clear that it was a very necessary motivation in his life.

Necessary, then, but is it enough? Clearly not. There are plenty of people with vision and conviction, especially in Christian service, who never seem to get anywhere. Having grown up in a missionary family and moved in Christian circles, I am only too aware of people who launch into things with conviction. Many are able to convince others of the potential of their dream and can attract significant levels of funding. But somehow things do not work out. Sometimes they never quite manage to build a viable team around themselves. Sometimes they never quite find the right plot of land. Sometimes they never quite seem to grasp the plot itself. The trouble with conviction, especially the conviction needed to overcome serious obstacles, is that its prime benefit is to meet and overcome difficulties, not to evaluate itself.

So how do we introduce some evaluation? There used to be one of those desk-signs that said, 'Those of you who think you know everything are a real pain to those of us who do.' Behind the sarcasm and irony lies that truth that some people just know when to back themselves (or others) while other people do not. Our convictions about ourselves are rarely a good guide as to the category to which we belong. However, a few people will simply know when to keep on backing their vision. I suspect that Daniel was like that. I would guess that the combination of his walk with God and his own experience in making difficult calls enabled him to understand that this next step was the one to take. For most of us, life is more difficult, and the New Testament, in particular, adds a couple of factors that may be helpful in deciding on a change in career.

We have already noted the importance of a track record of some sort and personal conviction. Jesus notes the importance of fruit: 'By their fruit you will recognize them. Do people pick grapes from thornbushes, or figs from thistles? Likewise every good tree bears good fruit, but a bad tree bears bad fruit. A good tree cannot bear bad fruit, and a bad tree cannot bear good fruit. Every tree that does not bear good fruit is cut down and thrown into the fire. Thus, by their fruit you will recognize them' (Matt 7:16-20). Paul's teaching on gifts is that we develop them by using them (Rom 12:3-8). While some enterprises will take a long time to mature, it is probably helpful to ask God for some early evidence of fruit in the endeavour. Early fruit is good evidence that we are starting on the right track.

The other useful piece of advice is not to make too many decisions entirely on our own. Acts 13:1-3 is perhaps the most obvious example of God providing guidance through a community of people. The recurring theme of team leadership for churches encourages us to get consensus, even over something as personal as the next step in our spiritual career. The advantages are obvious – others will see a bigger picture: 'Plans fail for lack of counsel, but with many advisers they succeed' (Prov 15:22). Apart from the fact that others will be able to see us as we cannot see ourselves, taking the church leadership with us should also enable our Christian spirituality to be factored into the equation.

A further development

Again, I don't want to rush through Daniel's prayer ministry, here. We need to take time to look at that properly. But in terms of his career, this seems to be the last development he experiences. And I think there is a special role for the elderly in praying for the rest of the church. I am not sure that it is simply a matter of time, or of filling those extra hours as our need for sleep declines. I think there is also something about appreciating what others are experiencing and having the insight, patience and charity that go with experience.

In our old church, there was a chap in his seventies who spent hours each day praying for the rest of us. In our present church, there is an octogenarian who prays for us all. You know that if you ask her to pray for something, it will be prayed for. She is diligent in following up on the things she is praying about and the fellowship is blessed as a result of her efforts.

I am only guessing, but it seems to me that simply getting older does not automatically create a ministry of prayer. There is something else there, and a church is fortunate if a significant number of its elderly people develop this ministry. It is something special and your church is in for blessing if you know someone with this ministry.

A structured career?

How, then, do we pull all this together? I started out by regarding Daniel as a great exemplar of the secular worker, one of the first Jews to forge what we would recognise as a career. Surprisingly, at the end we discover him treading a well-beaten path as a visionary committed to praying for his people. While his forefathers might not have understood what his early years were all about, most would probably have understood the latter visions and prayer life in fairly conventional terms.

In trying to follow his journey ourselves we, too, can trace a trajectory that says something in our generation. Daniel has a successful career and, as that wanes, finds himself engaged in new ministries, first in terms of his visions and later in terms of intercessory prayer. It doesn't decouple quite that cleanly, since he is quite likely to be back in royal service during the last glimpses we get of him – but there is something of a pattern to his life.

In our day, we find that many Christians have the opportunity either to ease off their careers or even formally to retire and move into new things. In many ways, Daniel provides a very up-to-date example to follow. The big question is, can we formalise the lessons in any useful way?

To some extent, missions and even churches have already started to do this. Many expect evidence of profitable secular experience before they will consider candidates for Christian service. While I accept there is room for exceptions, it seems to me to be an excellent policy. Maybe it is just that I am getting older, but I sense a trend with pastors, vicars, ministers and so forth, to have had a significant career in some sphere unrelated to their faith before moving into full-time service.

However, the transition is still the exception, rather than the rule. The number of Christians taking early retirement, or enjoying increased leisure time and resources, is not matched by anything like a comparable number moving into Christian service in any formal way. How might we formalise it?

This will hardly sound like rocket science, but it seems to me that the trick is not to jump too many fences at once, and to leave room for testing each move before consolidating and moving on. I do not want to propose a formula, because it really will be different for everyone. I just want people to think seriously that the normal Christian development might be to build onto a solid period of workplace experience, a growing ministry or set of ministries with God.

So, for instance, finding a role within the church in your spare time might enable you to test (with others) whether your gifts match your role or aspirations. There is no sense packing in your job to become a youth worker if you do not even know how you will get on with the young people. However, if helping to run a youth event once a month works out well, maybe a further step is justified. Again, having tested the waters, maybe it is time to take the chance to reduce the hours and go part-time. Maybe that will provide time for extra training while still generating funds for survival as well as the training. And then, if the service is really roaring ahead, maybe it is time to take the big plunge.

In any realistic example, it is not going to work out that simply. Often we do not face a set of clear, well-timed decisions. Often we will have to step out in faith or lose the opportunity. But looking back, I would be surprised if we could not identify some of the preparatory work in our lives. There are a couple of questions at the end to help you explore these ideas.

In the end…

Perhaps the most forcible message from Daniel about careers, is that they have a very short shelf life. At the end of the day the ministries they spawn are much more important.

I hope you find this both surprising and obvious. There can be few careers quite as glittering as Daniel's or pursued with more diligence and wisdom. As an example of working through difficult situations, or surviving in ambiguous circumstances, Daniel's career is an immensely rewarding study. But ultimately, it is the ministries that emerge from his secular career that have really endured.

Today we are very aware of our careers. Daniel would probably have struggled even to recognise our concept of a career. We lavish time and effort on our careers – not simply in preparing and planning for them – but in the many nights we work late; the boring events outside of work we attend; the residential weekends we squeeze into our bursting schedules. For many, particularly men, to be without a job is to be stripped of meaning or value. I noticed this during my one encounter with unemployment. No job, no role in life.

So what really matters about us? Perhaps the greatest tragedy is where we think one element of our lives – one type of achievement, one facet of our personalities – is what really matters, when actually it is something else. Sir Richard Burton, the Victorian explorer, longed to be in demand over his travelogues and geographical discoveries. Although he discovered the source of the Nile and guessed correctly that there was a linguistic link between gypsies and India, he was never successful when writing about the things he cared about most. Burton's skill was languages. He claimed to be able to pick up a new language in about six weeks, but his real genius lay in being able to move on to speak without an accent and to drop seamlessly into the customs and culture of a new people group. Needless to say, this led to a restless life in pursuit of new languages and cultures to master (usually while on sick leave from the forces).

While Burton felt the public would be interested in his adventures, discoveries and conjectures, the public taste for unusual places and new customs turned out to be entirely satiable. It was only towards the end of his life that he started applying his genius in a different way in a new career as a translator. It was Burton who first brought us the *Arabian Nights* and would have brought us the *Karma Sutra* had his wife (a devout Catholic) not been horrified to read what her husband had been translating and burned much of his work after his death. At the very end of his life he was working on some poems in an obscure Italian dialect that he had learned as a teenager. In many ways, Burton is quite a tragic character, wanting to be recognised for one set of achievements, but actually remembered for something else. If only he had sorted it out much earlier in his life and made the match between what he had to offer and what the public wanted. For many of us, there is that same tension between where we can make a great contribution and where we would like to make it.

I came across this passage recently (Ezek 15:2-5): 'Son of man, how is the wood of a vine better than that of a branch on any of the trees in the forest? Is wood ever taken from it to make anything useful? Do they make pegs from it to hang things on? And after it is thrown on the fire as fuel and the fire burns both ends and chars the middle, is it then useful for anything? If it was not useful for anything when it was whole, how much less can it be made into something useful when the fire has burned it and it is charred?'

Put this next to Jesus teaching on vines (John 15:5-8): 'I am the vine; you are the branches. If a man remains in me and I in him, he will bear much fruit; apart from me you can do nothing. If anyone does not remain in me, he is like a branch that is thrown away and withers; such branches are picked up, thrown into the fire and burned. If you remain in me and my words remain in you, ask whatever you wish, and it will be given you. This is to my Father's glory, that you bear much fruit, showing yourselves to be my disciples.'

What I do not know about vines can be found in most elementary texts – vines are not my territory. I think it is interesting that Jesus calls his followers to be branches of a vine and yet Ezekiel notes that the wood from a vine is pretty well useless – you cannot build anything with it nor is it much of a fuel. In fact, a reviewer helpfully pointed out to me that the Old Testament is not that positive about vines at all (e.g. Psa 80:8-19; Isa 5:1-7)!

So what is important about the vine? Clearly this is an important question for vines to resolve about themselves. The answer of course is that the vine itself is only valuable to the extent that it bears fruit. Hey, but what fruit! And the wine that comes from the fruit may sell for a fortune and last for ages. But you cannot get the wine without the vine.

It is a nice paradox – something that is next to useless, yields something of such lasting value. I think the simple farming illustration about the vine and its fruit is helpful when we look at Daniel. Impressive as his CV looks, it is as nothing next to his ministry before God. Ultimately the glittering career must give birth to something more valuable. And I am sure that Daniel really understood that.

We may find it hard to take that lesson properly on board. The things we want to be remembered for are probably quite different from the things God wants from our lives. So many Christians want to market themselves as good building material, excellent for high quality furniture, or as high-energy combustibles for those cold winter mornings. And God just wants fruit.

And what Daniel tells us is that those valuable ministries are connected in some way with our secular work. We will explore this later in a little more detail, but I think there is a strong encouragement here to seek the ministry with at least the same diligence as we have pursued the career.

And I think this sets the pattern for Christian life. The physical must give way to the spiritual. Christian life is a continuous process of development in which new ministries grow up out of a physical existence that must fade. Ultimately, the things we strive for have to give way to fruit, or our lives are wasted. 'Therefore we do not lose heart. Though outwardly we are wasting away, yet inwardly we are being renewed day by day. For our light and momentary troubles are achieving for us an eternal glory that far outweighs them all. So we fix our eyes not on what is seen, but on what is unseen. For what is seen is temporary, but what is unseen is eternal' (2 Cor 4:16-18).

Thinking it through

1. A Christian friend confides that he is keen to teach young people. He is intelligent and articulate and can plan things out in great detail, but in a couple of trial sessions, he does not succeed in holding the attention of teenagers. How do you help when he comes to you for advice?

2. A couple in their late twenties tell the church that they want to go to Bible school. You and your wife are asked, with another couple, to interview them and report back to

the annual church meeting. As part of your preparation, you discover that neither is getting on very well at work. How would you like to explore this issue in the interview?

3. What resources in the over-50s group is your church failing to use? How might it exploit such resources to greater blessing all around?

4. How does the world around us expect our usefulness to change as we age?

5. A friend of yours has just been bitterly disappointed in missing out for a promotion she had set her heart upon. How would you turn the situation over when she comes around for dinner later that week?

6. A hospital manager and his wife (a consultant surgeon) have opted to retire early from the NHS to spend 5 years working in a Christian hospital overseas. How might you explore their plans with them?

7. In the end, this couple set out, with the full blessing, support and prayers of your church. At first it all seems to be going swimmingly. However, a year and a half later, the mission committee at church starts to receive worrying e-mails. There are two problems. First, your friends discover that the local mission organisation has such a democratic approach to the hospital that your friends are unable to make any significant decisions, even though they are held responsible for the running of the hospital. Second, the local church, with which the hospital has traditionally worked closely, is undergoing a split. A few 'phone calls reveal that your friends are the third team to hit problems at this hospital in five years. How might you proceed?

8. A friend in her fifties has recently reduced her hours and has found time to support the toddler's group at church as a cheerful listener. She has been invited around for coffee by several of the mothers and wonders whether a ministry is developing. How might you advise?

9. A change in the job market has finally left a technically well-qualified member of your home group almost unemployable. He asks for special prayer and you meet with him to listen to his difficulties. It becomes clear that he is looking to you for some ideas on what to do next. How might you explore the future?

10. How would you know when to try something new, and when to stick with the career you have?
11. How might your church seek to develop more people in a ministry of prayer? How might you select suitable candidates and develop their gifts in this area?
12. Why do you think Jesus uses the metaphor of the vine in his teaching, since it had such a bad press in the Old Testament? How does Jesus set about rescuing, transforming and rehabilitating this metaphor? How is this characteristic of his wider ministry?

4

God at work

So far, we have looked at life from Daniel's perspective. But what was God up to in all this, and why? Were God's purposes purely for the exiled Jews and was it just a case of waiting until they had learned their lesson before returning to life as usual back in their homeland? Is this a bit like any other parent, getting on with life, while their disobedient child sits on the stairs for ten minutes and then goes back to play once more?

The evidence is that God plans to be more active, rather than less active about the place, following the exile of his people. Before this, God has focused his love and attention on a rather minor group of people. Now God has plans for the superpower that has captured them. Scripture is full of this kind of divine perversity – those who seek to preserve their lives lose them, while those who lose their lives are the ones who gain them (Luke 17:33); the corn seed must die before it can live (John 12:24).

What about the miracles?

As soon as we start to look at life in the palace, we have records of miraculous happenings and visions that peer way, way into the future. For many readers of Daniel, the nature and the number of miracles here may present a difficulty. It is not as though they are easily taken out, either, since the stories are meaningless without them. Why tell a story of conscientious defiance, if Shadrach, Meshach and Abednego are not rescued for their faith? Why tell the story of the lions, if Daniel never makes it from the den? The narrator weaves the miraculous deeply into the tale, making it very hard to unpick. The fire through which Shadrach, Meshach and Abednego walk freely, consumes their jailers (Dan 3:22,25). The ravenous lions fast for a night before their breakfast frenzy an hour or two after dawn (Dan 6:23,24).

And I am not sure I can really help you out on the miracle front. Polkinghorne probably presents the best scientific and up-to-date perspective on the side of the angels. If you are into that world, his appeal to superconductivity as an analogy is helpful. Basically, certain metals or alloys display very normal resistive behaviour until you cool them below a certain temperature. Suddenly in the cooled environment, you enter a whole new world where things that should not happen, happen routinely and reproducibly. Currents flow forever without batteries to renew them. Perhaps miracles are a bit like that – you have entered a new domain where the unexpected has become normal.

I find CS Lewis least useful when he is trying hardest (and most illuminating where he addresses a topic in passing) and am not sure whether his treatise on miracles will help you or not. I found it quite hard work, although he is helpful in trying to explore the sorts of miracles we might believe in, once we accept that miracles are possible. Accepting that miracles can take place is not carte blanche acceptance of everyone's claims on miracles. Perhaps I should just encourage you to read a bit more Chesterton. He has a way of turning everything upside down, and then inviting you to stand on your head beside him to admire the view. I don't suppose it matters much which of his books you start with – *The Everlasting Man* is as good a place to start as any.

Theologically, I take the Bible as a whole and accept that if I am to deal with Almighty God, I am not in a position to tell him what he can and cannot do within his own creation. And if you pushed me, I would work back from Jesus Christ, whose life is inextricably miraculous, on through the rest of Scripture. From within the book of Daniel, however, I find that the characters act in very sane ways when they do things that I can recognise from my world. Indeed, they often do them exceptionally well. And woven in with this are some of the most miraculous events in Scripture. I understand the tensions of accepting these stories as true. For me the tensions of trying to cut them out are even more difficult to handle. So we'll push on with the stories as they have been written down for us.

First moves

The first blip on Nebuchadnezzar's radar screen comes when he interviews the latest batch of apprentices as they complete their training. Daniel and his friends attract the king's attention because of the excellence of their answers.

However, his first real encounter with someone more powerful than himself comes when he has his dream about the statue with its head of gold (Dan 2:31-35). While he probably has the ego to identify himself with that head of gold, there is the distressing rock, hewn-out, but not by humans, that smashes the statue to dust and the wind that blows it away. Presumably there is some bad news in this dream. Since his magicians and wise men are not keen on delivering bad news to kings, he needs to be sure they are not just buttering him up if they come up with a good news theme.

And so he makes his bizarre demand – tell me the dream and then interpret it. We have already noted that the king is probably wary of their standard answer, but it creates a difficult environment for his specialists. The wise men are soon backed into a take-it-or-leave-it position since, 'No one can reveal it to the king except the gods, and they do not live among men' (Dan 2:11). Show us and we will show you. Tell us your dream and we will tell you the meaning.

Nebuchadnezzar is clearly unnerved as well as haunted by the dream and orders the execution of this entire cadre of privileged and valuable people. But when the interpretation comes the news is mixed. First, 'there is a God in heaven' (Dan 2:28) who has something to say to the king. I wonder how Nebuchadnezar would have received this news. Perhaps he would be concerned that, with all his enchanters and astrologers, he had missed out on this deity. Perhaps he thought this meant there was another base he needed to cover – rather like the Athenians with their extra altar, just in case they had missed someone out (Acts 17:23). Perhaps it had something to do with these Hebrews he was in the process of integrating into his empire. Good job he spotted Daniel back at that interview. Anyhow, what is the dream about?

Was he spooked as Daniel recounted the story? Ah yes, he got the bit about the rock and the dust that blew away in the wind. Now, when will all this happen? Daniel cannot have been long into his interpretation when Nebuchadnezzar is reassured. A dynasty of silver to follow his dynasty of gold! Sounds like he has a future! Not only that, but his kingdom stands head and shoulders above the rest! And finally Daniel gets to the rock that comes from nowhere. Although it does not seem a threat to Nebuchadnezzar in any immediate way, God is planning something that will fill the whole earth (Dan 2:35). Nebuchadnezzar understands dynasties, and this God is talking dynasties. He wants to let Nebuchadnezzar know that a dynasty is coming that will extend further than his own and last into eternity. It will destroy the others and endure forever.

Nebuchadnezzar's reaction is astonishing. He prostrates himself and promotes Daniel (Dan 2:46-48). He orders that offerings be made to him. Later on in the book, Daniel is described as a man in whom the spirit of the holy gods exist (Dan 4:8,9; 5:11), and presumably the king is worshipping the gods he believes live in Daniel's body. Despite the fact that Daniel has pointed out that the dream was beyond mortals (or perhaps because of it) Nebuchadnezzar seems to adopt this model of live-in deities and does obeisance accordingly. Daniel's denials that he is anything special are wasted. A piece of insight, however, is the way in which Nebuchadnezzar talks in terms of one God, identifying him as the God of gods and the Lord of kings (Dan 2:47). Overall, it is not hard to see why Daniel receives such swift promotion.

Perhaps it is Daniel's unusual position that prevents him from being shopped when his friends are hauled before Nebuchadnezzar over the golden image (Dan 3). Perhaps no-one wants to push their luck with Daniel.

Strategic manoeuvre

I have no idea why Nebuchadnezzar puts up the golden image. It could just be the everyday act of an absolute monarch. A quick review of totalitarian regimes over the past fifty years shows that the practice has survived to modern times and that the modern dictator is as keen to fill the land with his image as any classical monarch. Most of us will have seen television images of Sadam Hussein's statue being pulled down in Iraq. It is one of the enduring television images of the war.

Perhaps Nebuchadnezzar believes that he had this new God on side. Maybe he feels the imagery needs to be taken out of his dreams and into the high street. A statue with a head of gold – why not? He is clearly in with these new gods. If you've got it, flaunt it.

And so the narrative winds on inexorably towards a confrontation, or rather towards the first confrontation. It has a whiff of a Clint Eastwood western about it, where the good guy is roughed up early on, only to return explosively to victory in the end. As we watch from outside the story we can see that things are not quite as they appear and sense that roughing up the three Hebrews is a poor move. However, while the finale is spectacular, it is not vengeful. Nebuchadnezzar's life is not threatened, but his greatest weapon – the ability to execute – has been shattered in his hands. He set out to execute these men because they would not worship him, as he demanded. In their outspoken response (3:16-18) Shadrach, Meshach and Abednego have explained that they worship someone who might well be minded to rescue them. However, if not, dying for their God is preferable to worshipping the image. He has tried two of the most potent weapons in his armoury – intimidation and execution – and the whole procedure has failed abjectly, spectacularly, and in front of everyone.

Not only that, but the king catches sight of someone else in the furnace, someone who looks like 'a son of the gods' (Dan 3:25). Whoever these gods are, they seem to be taking an unusual and surprising interest in Babylon these days. This is the first time that Nebuchadnezzar has been forcibly prevented from doing something. The negative and the positive elements of this tour de force are not wasted on him. He is lavish in his response and grants the God of Shadrach, Meshach and Abednego significant legal standing (Dan 3:28,29).

God's aim in all this is not to crush Nebuchadnezzar. From day one, the people sent his way have been a blessing to him, competent, insightful and hardworking. Daniel's interpretation of the king's first dream stresses that the power he exercises is a gift from God. And it seems that Nebuchadnezzar is unable fully to understand what his relationship with God should be. Worship him? Certainly! Let's make sure there is plenty of incense, and we will worship at his altar, too. Alongside the other gods, there will certainly be room for Daniel's God. Whoops! Maybe we have overstepped with Shadrach, Meshach and Abednego. Better put something in the regulations to make sure it does not happen again. Perhaps Nebuchadnezzar does not even link the two episodes as encounters with the same God.

Faith on the menu

Nebuchadnezzar is king and life goes on the way he wants it to. He is jolly appreciative of the surprising new support he has been receiving. He may need to watch his P's and Q's at times, but otherwise, the world is very much his oyster.

For many people, this is a common way to see God. In a patchwork of influences, gods and superstitions, they are glad to be able to pray when they need to. Perhaps there have even been crunch points – prayers uttered in desperation and in isolation, times that no-one else knows about – and maybe God has answered. Maybe against the odds, the illness faded or the next phase never came. Perhaps, surprisingly, the spouse came back and made a real go of the marriage and with the family. Maybe the situation at work miraculously improved, maybe a wonderful neighbour moved in to break the tedium of existence or to stand against intimidation on the estate. Maybe God worked through people who worshipped him alone but now it is time to move on. Nevertheless, God will always have a special place in our life.

And in one sense it is not surprising that people feel this way. So often God is presented as an insurance policy in case of difficult times. Too often our evangelistic patter involves the way God helps us out; the way God makes us feel; the way God increases our chances of success. Of course people will have some of that. And they will have some of the other, too. Why not? In a menu-driven society, by all means, let's have some Christianity on the menu. And I honestly don't blame people for feeling that way.

But the first problem is that life isn't really like that. There are some things you can't have a bit of – you either have them or you don't. There is a story about a Count whose wife asked him whether he had been faithful. 'Frequently, my dear, frequently,' was the response. The irony in the tale, of course is that 'faithful' and 'frequently' do not really mix. And it is that way with God – he does not mix well. For Nebuchadnezzar, it will turn out to be 'either this or that', not 'this and that'.

The second difficulty with a menu-driven faith is that it makes few real demands upon us. It is a rah-rah approach to life. Nebuchadnezzar can be as arrogant as he pleases. He has no real responsibilities in life. He is accountable to no-one. But life with God can never be that independent. And so the next step in Nebuchadnezzar's journey into faith is a really painful kicking.

Now why do that? If God's main purpose is to demonstrate that he can protect Daniel and his fellow exiles throughout the years of captivity, the goal has been reached. If the goal is to demonstrate that the city went down but that the God over the city is still alive and well – then that, too, has been achieved. Remember the concerns we raised as Daniel trudged into exile? Would his God be able to look after him? The answer is clear – of course! The worries are already revealed as flimsy and insubstantial concerns.

So why bother? Well, I think there are two reasons. First, God is really interested in Nebuchadnezzar. He is committed to breaking through and fulfilling the wonderful future he has hinted at for Nebuchadnezzar. Most of us are comfortable with the idea that there is no-one too small for God, no-one too insignificant to miss out on his care. However, most of us secretly believe that there are many people who are too big for God – too important to really need him, too influential, perhaps even too powerful, to attract his attention. And that is not true.

How much of our time really goes into praying seriously and meaningfully for the powerful in our world? What does Paul say? 'I urge, then, first of all, that requests, prayers, intercession and thanksgiving be made for everyone – for kings and all those in authority, that we may live peaceful and quiet lives in all godliness and holiness. This is good, and pleases God our Saviour, who wants all men to be saved and to come to a knowledge of the truth' (1 Tim 2:1-4).

Second, all those bits about salvation for the whole world were really true. God really meant that great promise to Abraham, 'And through your offspring all nations on earth will be blessed' (Gen 22:18). 'All nations will be blessed through him, and they will call him blessed' (Psa 72:17b). Isaiah is tuned in to the same message: 'I will also make you a light for the Gentiles, that you may bring my salvation to the ends of the earth' (Isa 49:6b). God's purposes stretch out and out.

It was one of the great discoveries that the New Testament writers made as they trawled their Old Testaments. Here is Paul getting excited: 'For I tell you that Christ has become a servant of the Jews on behalf of God's truth, to confirm the promises made to the patriarchs so that the Gentiles may glorify God for his mercy, as it is written: "Therefore I will praise you among the Gentiles; I will sing hymns to your name." Again, it says, "Rejoice, O Gentiles, with his people." And again, "Praise the Lord, all you Gentiles, and sing praises to him, all you peoples." And again, Isaiah says, "The Root of Jesse will spring up, one who will arise to rule over the nations; the Gentiles will hope in him"' (Rom 15:8-12).

God's ability to shock and surprise us with the scale of his plans is one of the great themes of Scripture. God is not out simply to protect Daniel, nor the cohort of people whom Daniel represents. His plans embrace the empire.

So what is Nebuchadnezzar's big problem? How about his human rights record? Isn't the real issue here that the king does not uphold the human rights of his subjects? Or perhaps the inequalities of the society he runs is the key problem. How many of us asked to sort Nebuchadnezzar out, would prescribe something on social justice, wealth redistribution, land rights for the dispossessed or a moratorium on the appalling loss of life through prolonged military campaigns? Important as these issues are, they tend to be issues that we are, on the whole, rather good at and that Nebuchadnezzar was rather poor at. The thing that matters to God is something that we are as bad at as Nebuchadnezzar was. In our humanistic society, by and large, we are very concerned about the things that happen to people. God is rather more concerned about people's attitude to the Almighty – and pride is the great sin in that world. CS Lewis' chapter on pride in *Mere Christianity* is perhaps the most perceptive and accessible exploration of the vice.

Pride does not look like much to us. We feel the unpalatable side of the arrogance of others but generally accept that personal pride is part of life. Pride drives the ambition that fuels our economic success. In fact, pride drives so many aspects of our life that it is very nearly invisible. Ezekiel catches a flavour of the problem from God's perspective:

> In the pride of your heart you say, "I am a god;
> I sit on the throne of a god in the heart of the seas."
> But you are a man and not a god, though you think you are
>   as wise as a god.
>
> (Ezek 28:2)

Body blow

The blow is softened for the reader by the style in which the story is related. We have a record from the king himself. So, whatever has happened, presumably the king is okay once again. For Nebuchadnezzar, the blow comes, at least, with a warning in the form of a dream (Dan 4:5). His dream is of a tree that grows until its top touches the sky and can be seen from the ends of the earth. Its leaves and fruit provide shelter and nourishment for animal herds and flocks of birds. And then the dream goes horribly wrong as the tree is hewn down and the stump left to rot in the rain for seven seasons (Dan 4:10-17). However, there is hope for the stump, which is protected by an iron band until it becomes fruitful once more.

My guess is that even the most junior trainee wizard would have recognised that this dream was very bad news indeed: bad news for the king and very bad news for the first person to break it to him. It is not surprising that they were unable to make anything of it (Dan 4:7). This time, Nebuchadnezzar knows that he has someone to whom he can turn, so he pulls Daniel into the loop.

Daniel sees all too clearly what the warning is about and tries desperately to steer the king towards a path of contrition and humility before God (4:27). It says much for his standing that he is not censured for the savagery of the prediction, nor for volunteering his advice to the king. As it is, the king genially ignores the advice of his favourite seer. A year later he is bragging, presumably to his retinue, about his achievements in Babylon, when the judgement falls. A single verse describes an appalling passage of his life when he goes insane and lives as an animal in the wild. While the brevity of the description is an excellent literary device and adds impact to the shocking narrative, it probably also reflects Daniel's horror at this unpalatable turn of events.

This morning I finished reading Frank Abagnale's *Catch me if you can*. I had heard Frank being interviewed on my way into work one morning when Spielberg's film was first released. A few months ago, my wife and I watched the video and then I saw the book on holiday and was intrigued to find out how much of the tale had been changed in the filming.

A period covered in much more detail in the book than the film, is his life in a couple of European jails, before he wound up imprisoned in the US. As I read, I was shocked at the inhumanity of his time at Perpignan. It was a punishment inflicted on him by other human beings within the past fifty years, and for six months he lived naked in a pitch black hole, covered in his own excrement, while his hair and beard grew like that of an animal. He reckons he would have died or gone insane had his initial sentence of a year been carried out in full. In the end, he was released early and went on to experience life at the other end of the penal spectrum in Sweden. Surprisingly, in an interview at the end of the book, he is not vengeful against the harsher system and believes it to have had some merits.

In a similar way, Nebuchadnezzar takes an unexpectedly positive view of his humiliation. When the king's sanity is restored, he sees God's hand in his own humiliation and restoration to power:

All the peoples of the earth are regarded as nothing.
He does as he pleases with the powers of heaven and the peoples of the earth.
No one can hold back his hand or say to him: "What have you done?"

(Dan 4:35)

Although the prescription is devastating, it works! Not only has Nebuchadnezzar had his own, life-changing encounter with God, but his paean of praise is sent out to, 'the peoples, nations and men of every language, who live in all the world' (Dan 4:1).

Now why should God resort to such desperate measures? My guess is that it is because our pride is about the most resistive barrier we can put up against the work of God in our lives. We have only to look at the line of brutal totalitarians thrown up over the past century to realise how destructive and unmanageable human pride can be. But there are modern examples of those who have fallen from high office into dire humiliation, only to discover that God is there at the end of their fall, ready to accept them and restore them to fruitful service. I have recently been reading some of Charles Colson's work. He was a senior player in President Nixon's administration who was jailed after Watergate. Not only is Charles converted, but a prison ministry in running Bible studies also opens up for him. Among his publications, *Loving God,* provides clear evidence of the permanence and depth of the change in his life, and is well worth reading if you get the opportunity. A more recent example in the

UK might be Jonathan Aitken, another political high-flier, who had a conversion experience connected to a spell in prison. His books, *Pride and Perjury* and *Porridge and Passion* bear moving tribute to the change in his life.

Such conversions are often viewed with a degree of cynicism. But let's not forget that scorn and mockery are the abrasives we use to polish our own pride. How does the Psalter open? 'Blessed is the man who does not walk in the counsel of the wicked or stand in the way of sinners or sit in the seat of mockers' (Psa 1:1).

Sadly, there are times when the cynics get it right. The conversion is just a flash in the pan. The candidate senses a freedom from the crushing guilt or shame and relaxes back into an easier, more accustomed lifestyle, rather like the seed that sprang up on the rocky places in the parable (Matt 13:5) and then wilted away. One of the most dramatic conversions I ever encountered was followed by a life that never quite shook free of the past. The last I heard, the poor fellow seemed to have lost it and was drifting slowly back into his old ways. But we must not let the setbacks undermine our appreciation of how far God is prepared to go to get through to us.

There are people whose first real encounter with God came after a major event in which they were made aware of their own powerlessness. I can think of a chap who survived an aeroplane crash, scrambling out and running from a disaster behind him. Others find God out of the ashes of wrecked marriages, failed business ventures, or even an encounter with the law. This type of biography has been reasonably popular over the past couple of decades, and half an hour's browsing in your local Christian bookshop should furnish plenty of material. If you want more fun, take a clipboard to church next time and find out what motivated the various people there in turning to Christ.

Before we move on, let us remember that throughout the engagement, God has sought to meet Nebuchadnezzar in terms he can understand. Does Nebuchadnezzar need wise men? Here are some bright young counsellors! Does he believe in dreams as a way into the future? Here is an interpreter of dreams par excellence! Is he a tough guy, well used to getting his own way? Here is a God who is also used to getting his own way.

To the faithful you show yourself faithful,

to the blameless you show yourself blameless,
to the pure you show yourself pure,
but to the crooked you show yourself shrewd.
You save the humble but bring low those whose eyes are
haughty.

(Psa 18:25-27)

Impact in prayer

Most readers of a book like this will already be converted. I don't see that my gift lies in making the evangelistic pitch to those outside the Christian faith and so I would expect most people reading this to be after something in their Christian lives. So why should all this matter? How should it change the lives of those who have already committed their lives to Christ?

Well, it may impact the way we pray for those in difficulty. Our knee-jerk reaction is to pray that the distressing circumstances will go away. Someone's neighbour has just been taken into hospital. 'Lord, heal her,' we all pray. It doesn't cost us much in thinking time and it seems like the right thing to do. But that isn't what Daniel does for Nebuchadnezzar. Although he is frankly horrified (Dan 4:19) by the humiliation on the horizon, he does not pray that God will take it away. He urges the king towards moral reform, but he does not pray for everything to turn out dandy. Daniel senses himself in an unusual position, poised between the God of heaven and the greatest ruler on earth. Such a path requires delicate footwork and will occasionally tear him apart. Clearly Daniel is torn by the news, but he possesses sufficient insight to appreciate that this is an experience the king must endure, and endure to his ultimate benefit, rather than avoid.

Surely the best thing we can pray for friends encountering difficult, even unpalatable times, is that they will find God in the experience. After all, as the narrative here shows so graphically, experiences pass, but our relationship to God is of eternal import. I sometimes wonder if God finds our prayer meetings a bit frustrating. He sets up a series of circumstances designed to bring someone to the end of himself or herself and to create a sense of need, and then the prayer meeting is alight with requests that the status quo be restored. We just want everything to be all right.

All right? I don't think so. So why do we pray this way?

First, I think we are lazy. I am certainly lazy in prayer and it is generally easier to pray easy things than to spend time asking God what is going on and how best to pray. I have had a busy day and collapse into bed, what is there to pray about? Well, let's pray about the first things that come into our heads. We have discussed all the things to pray about for the past twenty minutes and now we have only ten minutes of our prayer meeting left – better make it brisk.

But I am not sure we even have a concept of thinking things through in prayer. We have a mentality that, basically, God wants everything to be fine for everyone and that a simple prayer for goodies all around will be the right one. I could go on about laziness in prayer for pages, but you are probably as lazy as I am and will benefit much more by putting the book down for five minutes and thinking about your own prayer life.

Second, I am not sure we fully believe in the goodness of God. How many of us could believe that this catastrophe could be evidence of God's goodness to the king? We are so used to snappy solutions (usually presented within a half-hour slot on television) that we have little concept of the long harsh road to recovery that begins with a very serious setback.

This certainly does not mean that we ought to judge those going through tough times. I think, like Daniel, we should be appalled at human suffering. Where we can, we have a responsibility to do something about it. Jonah wants the judgement to fall on the people to whom he is sent (Jonah 4:2) – and Jonah is a very unsatisfactory prophet. Nor does it mean that we ought to seek out the high moral ground, explaining blandly that this is for their own good.

It is a bit paradoxical, but I believe we can pray the difficult prayer that God will bring good out of trying circumstances, rather than the simple prayer that he will make everything okay. It is the way Jesus prayed about his own suffering in Gethsemane: 'My Father, if it is possible, may this cup be taken from me. Yet not as I will, but as you will' (Matt 26:39). Paul also encourages us to look for great good even in the most severe circumstances: 'And we know that in all things God works for the good of those who love him, who have been called according to his purpose' (Rom 8:28).

Finally, I am not sure we really grasp the greatness of God. We find it hard to believe, but the important thing is not what happens to us, but what happens to the name of God, 'for the earth will be full of the knowledge of the LORD as the waters cover the sea' (Isa 11:9b). Above everything else, Daniel shows us that God is concerned about his global reputation.

Why else wreck Belshazzar's party (Dan 5:5)? Nebuchadnezzar's reign is a distant memory and this upstart king is having a ball to divert his attention from the besieging armies. He has plundered the treasury containing gold and silver goblets from the old temple in Jerusalem so that a thousand of his nobles may drink in style. He has no concern for this God of Israel and he is very open in the way he despises all things Jewish. He even reminds Daniel, when he finally meets him, that he is an exile, brought under compulsion to Babylon.

Now why wreck the party? The river has been diverted. That very night the Medes and Persians will march up the dry riverbed and into Babylon itself. The message on the wall is not a message of warning. It is a judgement. Belshazzar is not being offered the second chance that Nebuchadnezzar was offered. The party is over for Belshazzar. He has shown his contempt for the God of Israel and the God of Israel has passed sentence. It has been a deadly game and now it is important that everyone recognises the winner. The message is simple – you do not play games with this God – and a thousand nobles from a dying regime saw and took notice.

It depends how you read the text, but if Darius in Daniel is the Cyrus we know, then not long afterwards, Belshazzar's successor, Cyrus issues a proclamation allowing the Jews to return to their land and commanding them to rebuild the temple. Was there a causal link between the two events? It is not even clear that Cyrus would have seen this as the seminal event recorded for us in Scripture. As far as Cyrus was concerned, this was standard policy.

I wonder whether those who had watched the finger writing on the wall that night made the connection? Maybe, from their perspective, there was more to it. Certainly the people who wrote it up and passed it down to us, felt there was an overarching purpose, a providential power, at work in their world.

It is hard to see the very broadest pattern of God's working in our own time. The minutiae are evident. People we know come to Jesus and their lives are changed. They learn to depend upon

God and some see surprising responses to their cries for help and guidance. But what is happening on the larger scale? As I say, it is very hard to see the pattern clearly. But there is one very obvious example. I grew up in a world in which one superpower had set itself against the very idea of God. I grew up with stories of a persecuted church behind the Iron Curtain. My Sunday school teacher even gave up his job to serve with his wife in supporting Christians behind the Iron Curtain, and eventually he wrote a book about his experiences (*Moving God's Finger* by Trevor Harris). And where is the consortium of nations that set itself against God and those who worshipped him, now? Dissipated! Where are the atheistic dictators? That generation has gone.

And so, despite the apparent failure at the fall of Jerusalem, God has shown himself freer than ever to take a hand in the affairs of state. He has shown himself willing to correct or condemn the potentates who rose to power and passed away. Over the coming decades, a steady stream of Jewish exiles exerts some influence in the palace of the superpower. And Daniel's prediction is that a much bigger surprise is in store.

Thinking it through

1. How could you use Daniel's approach to Nebuchadnezzar as a template for praying for a friend of yours?

2. Your next-door neighbour, who has been hostile to you for several years, has just been diagnosed with cancer. What would you say on first hearing this serious news, and how would you proceed from there?

3. A friend from a local church that believes very strongly in healing has had bowel cancer for some time and is not being healed. Her pastor has told her she lacks the faith to be healed – how might you work through this with her when she comes around for coffee?

4. Paul urges us to pray for those in authority (1 Tim 2:1,2). What specific prayers would be appropriate today?

5. To what extent is the church you worship at, a bit too influential?

6. Has Isaiah's vision of the glory of God covering the earth as the waters cover the sea (Isa 11:9) advanced or retreated

in the past fifty years?

7. Does God deal with nations as nations, or is the appeal of the Gospel today purely to individuals? Develop your answer.

8. How many stories can you gather about God's dealings with global political figures in the past 20 years?

9. How would you describe the attitude of most Christians to communist leaders in the past 40 years? In the light of Daniel, to what extent has this approach been helpful?

10. How do you think Daniel might have fared as a senior advisor to a government behind the Iron Curtain in the mid-'70s?

11. If Godless governments fall in the end, does Daniel lead us to believe this says anything special about those administrations that remain?

12. How has God been working on your pride in the last 6 months?

5

The vision thing

As I mentioned in the introduction, there is a tendency to separate the visions from the rest of Daniel. In terms of understanding the book, this leads to a bizarre split, where the stories from the first half of the book are considered suitable for the youngest listener, while the visions are PhD material. That one book should embrace such diverse tastes is noteworthy, but the dividing line is a little disconcerting. Is there no way into the second half of the book that is accessible to everyone? In terms of an everyday approach, it would be nice to break through the barrier that makes Daniel a book of two halves. Not that you have to, necessarily, but it might be nice to try.

I think you can, in a very general way, do just that. To do this, I may lump several things together that you might consider quite separate. You may or may not be happy with the result. If you feel I have been a bit too free, by all means sit down and work your way into the book for yourself – there is much greater reward in finding your own way around the material, than there is in reading mine. However, I'm enjoying myself writing this as I sit beside the pool on holiday and watch the family having fun. So let's see how far I can get before I need to cool off, too.

I believe that there are several ways in which this new phase of Daniel's ministry links to the old. First, it seems to me that Daniel's first dream starts in the same sort of territory as the first dream he had to interpret for Nebuchadnezzar. That this new venture should link all the way back to his first major success in the court at Babylon, over thirty years earlier, must have encouraged him that this ministry was going in the right direction. A second link is the way in which the type of vision that Daniel has is so closely tied to the career he has enjoyed in political strategy. If, for instance, we compare Daniel's visions with Ezekiel, the exile whose prophecy precedes Daniel's in our Bibles, we find very a very different character, with a very different set of interests who had a very different type of vision.

Whether this turns out to be a fruitful pursuit, you will have to decide, but I think it is interesting to look at what we know of Daniel's personality and skills and to see how they are reflected in the type of vision he has. This, of course, raises some interesting questions if you believe that visions are revelations dictated directly from heaven. If you see the Old Testament prophets as early word-processors, recording verbatim a stream of words from somewhere else, you may not see any value in the exercise. However, if you believe that God's plan is to involve the prophet and that God is able to use the background and skills of the prophet in speaking to his people, then you might find this a worthwhile endeavour.

And so an interesting question is whether vision, in its broadest sense, can be linked to our experience and areas of competence. I like strategy, and it seems to me that Daniel has something to say about it. However, and we will try to return to this in the end, the book of Daniel is about God's interactions with people. Most of the picture is painted on a very broad canvas, but it is a human canvas, nonetheless. If it doesn't speak to us as people, our efforts are wasted.

So what were Daniel's dreams and visions about? He has already interpreted the king's dream in chapter 2 – a dream about a statue with a head of gold, arms of silver, torso and thighs of bronze, legs of iron and feet that were partly iron and partly clay. The first of his own visions is of a restless sea that throws up four monsters (chapter 7). A couple of years later, he has a second vision, this time about a ram and a goat. The final vision is a sort of interview with a man wearing a linen garment and a golden belt, which starts in chapter 10 and goes into great detail about the future in chapter 11. If you aren't familiar with what happens in these passages, it might be worth reading through them now.

Patterns in the visions

This whole field is full of perplexing material and I am certainly not saying that the approach I propose to follow is the best, most obvious, or only way of looking at it. The approach I suggest here is unlikely to attract critical acclaim today, although it follows, in broad outline, the sort of sense the early Christian writers would have made of it, and I hope it will be helpful. It seems to me that the dreams and visions in which Daniel is involved cover the same passage of future history for the most part, revisiting or magnifying the scope as the visions develop. If we take this approach, we end up with something like the comparison shown in the table:

	Nebuchadnez-zar's deam	Daniel's first vision/dream	Daniel's second vision/dream	Daniel's last vision/dream
Babylonians	gold	winged lion		
Medes & Persians	silver	ravenous bear	ram	
Greeks	bronze	flying leopard	goat	lots of kings
Romans	iron, iron & clay	terrifying beast		
Chapter	2	7	8	(10&) 11
Daniel's age	Early twenties?	Fifties?	Early sixties?	Late eighties?

On this reading, Daniel's first dream covers the same four kingdoms as Nebuchadnezzar's – the Babylonians, the Medes and Persians (as a single kingdom), the Greeks and then the Romans. But I think it's time for a swim now.

Ah! That's better. Daniel's view is that there are four major kingdoms and then something major happens. Now I am not sure the details are critical in fitting all this together. The scheme above is neat, perhaps a little too neat, in closing the age and opening something new in the time of the Romans – and indeed, you don't have to do this for the ideas in either this chapter or the next to work. As I understand it, it is all a bit messy however you look at it – and most commentators today would, I understand, wind up with the Greeks as the fourth kingdom. The fact that there are four kingdoms was probably more important to Daniel than trying to tie them down. Four kingdoms, four winds. Four was quite an important number and surfaces again in Revelation.

Four kingdoms, and then something major... Actually, the

expression is rather more vague – the something comes, 'in the time of those kings' (Dan 2:44). It makes a neat match if we flatten out the statue, so to speak, into a sequence, because we are then, as we have just observed, in Roman times when Jesus is born. But it could be that something is happening throughout these kingdoms – it may already have started. There is some good evidence that it has, and that is why it may not matter if we do not manage to tie up all the loose ends, or if we find ourselves with a kingdom or two to spare.

For us, of course, as Christians, the major something is a major someone – the incarnation, God becoming human in the person of Jesus Christ. As he promised, Jesus builds his church (Matt 16:18), a new feature on the landscape that initially becomes sufficiently significant to engage the interest of secular rulers and ultimately transcends all political kingdoms.

As noted, the fact that his own first encounter as a visionary follows the same outline as that first dream he decoded decades earlier, must have been a great encouragement to Daniel. Four kingdoms and then the 'saints of the Most High will receive the kingdom and possess it forever' (Dan 7:18). In both dreams, the 'four nation' interpretation is explicitly confirmed (Dan 2:36-45; 7:17). This time, however, there is more detail, and personalities begin to emerge. In fact, there is a steady trend throughout the sequence of the four visions, as outlined in the table, to have ever more detail, greater focus and more emphasis on the people behind the movements.

In moving from Nebuchadnezzar's dream to Daniel's first vision, for example, we see the impersonal head of gold is represented instead as a brute of a flying lion that has his wings torn off. He is made to stand on his hind legs and receives the heart of a man. Surely these acts of taming and humanising hint at the great Nebuchadnezzar. Perhaps the four-headed flying leopard (Dan 7:6) hints at the four generals who divided up the world that Alexander the Great conquered. The picture becomes even more detailed and developed as we move to the next vision, where the goat's single horn is broken and four horns grow up in its place (Dan 8:8). Again, in Daniel's second vision, we may catch our first sight of Antiochus Epiphanes (Dan 8:23-25), a godless tyrant, who went further than any before him to desecrate the Jewish temple, and who was violently opposed through the guerrilla campaigns of the Maccabees. Indeed, as I understand it, most scholars see the central message of Daniel focusing on the conflict between Antiochus and the Jews and understand the prophecy as having been designed to give them strength in that most trying of times.

So even in Daniel's first vision, the rather static kingdoms of Nebuchadnezzar's dream are starting to be fleshed out here and there with hints of real people. The detail is being filled in. Can we also detect a slight change in perspective? There is a lot more heavenly activity about the place in Daniel's first dream than in Nebuchadnezzar's. Nor is the Ancient of Days in any way equivalent to the beasts. He does not fight with the beasts (although his saints do) but rather passes judgement against them (Dan 7:22, 26 and 27). I hope I am not being too imaginative here, but while Nebuchadnezzar's dream takes a very human perspective, and views things as he might have seen them, this new dream seems to see both things that happen on earth and things that happen in a heavenly realm.

These themes seem to develop in the ensuing dreams. The vision of the ram with its two horns and the goat that it defeated, develops more of the detail than the previous dream through the horns that grow up, and makes explicit the link between the saints and the beautiful land, on the one hand, and the goings-on in the heavenly realm on the other (Dan 8:9-14; 23-25). On the scheme outlined above we are in the Greek period as Alexander the Great defeats the Medo-Persian empire. We whiz through his stunning but brief career and then attention swings to the fate of Palestine and the Seleucids who came to rule them. Someone (Antiochus Epiphanes?) is in view (8:9-12; 23-25), interfering with temple worship and, eventually, desecrating the temple. By the time we reach the last dream, it is all detail. There are no images, beasts or animals, just oblique references to a sequence of kings. Bewildering detail, that is all.

Once the overall framework has been set in Nebuchadnezzar's dream and Daniel's first dream, the focus closes. In Daniel's second dream or vision, we concentrate on just two of the four kingdoms and the final vision reviews in considerable detail just part of the end of the Greek era as it affects Palestine. Neither Daniel's second nor third visions conclude in the cataclysmic manner of the first. However, in each case, God smashes the evil of the rulers of the day.

There is one further trend worth observing and that is the

degree to which a geographic element is introduced. Nebuchadnezzar's statue could be anywhere. The 'four winds of heaven' (Dan 7:2), provide some sense of orientation in Daniel's first dream, but the landscape is still rather amorphous and placeless. The terrain is just a churning sea – the same restless waves wherever you look. However, by the time we reach the ram and the goat, there is a sense of territory. Even Daniel has a vantage point for his vision – beside the Ulai Canal (Dan 8:2). The ram stakes out his territory by charging, 'toward the west and the north and the south' (Dan 8:4). The horn that grows up, waxes 'to the south and to the east and toward the Beautiful Land' (Dan 8:9). By the time we are in the last vision in chapter 11, the positional and directional indicators are everywhere – the king of the North, the king of the South, Egypt, the coastlands.

Here, then, we have a sequence of dreams and visions. The early dreams set a framework that is explored in greater detail by the later revelations. The framework stretches out a long way ahead. In fact, eventually, these visions present something eternal, something that lasts forever. The New Testament writers see elements of Daniel's dreams that still lie in the future – for instance, the abomination that causes desolation (compare Dan 9:27; 11:31; 12:11 with Matt 24:15 and Mark 13:14) towards the end of the life of the temple and even the end of all time. The framework involves a repeated pattern of kingdoms rising and being replaced by new kingdoms on earth. However, the main structural element of this framework is that God will intervene in human affairs. The rock from nowhere becomes a mountain and fills the earth (Dan 2:35). The saints possess the kingdom forever (Dan 7:18).

The last two visions explore parts of the framework – in increasing levels of detail. We catch sight of people, some of whom are household names even now, two and a half millennia later (depending, of course, on exactly how you read the text). Meanwhile, we become ever more aware that the dreams take in a lot of territory as well as stretching into the future, they spread out sideways. Not only does Daniel see way, way ahead, he sees new borders far, far away.

One last perspective, that may help in addressing the mind-numbing level of detail in chapter 11 is to think of it as an example of drilling down from the higher level detail presented earlier. One of the difficulties with strategy is that not everyone's mind works at that level. I am not saying that the high level view is best and not everyone who espouses a high level view is necessarily capable of really taking it in. The trick is to connect the high level vision with the practicalities of everyday life. The company director who wants to reposition her firm away from retailing clothes for grown-ups to trendy stuff for teenagers clearly needs to have a vision. Why does she think she can survive in the teenage market better than the incumbents? What is it that her firm offers that is new or cannot readily be replicated by the competition?

But she will also have to drill-down and explain in specific detail what it will mean for the people who produce the new garments, who pack them and who select the outlets that will sell them. She may need, for instance, to convert the vision into a goal of selling everything in sets of items that lie below a certain cost threshold (£20?), or that can be bought individually but can be worn in mix-and-match combinations. There may be specifics in terms of finish that need discussing with the machinists. The director does not need to have the full picture in view, but experienced directors will drill down in specific areas to satisfy themselves that the strategy can be implemented and to do this, they will seek a great deal of detail. The challenge, in industry and in our churches is that few people are gifted with an eye for the big picture and an ability to manage the details. Daniel appears to have had the skill to manage the wide sweep and the focused study. That is the tension of his dreams. It may well have been a key contributor to his political success.

However, Daniel's detail is not there to satisfy himself that the vision holds together in quite the same way, but the drill-down provides a perspective that will help people when they encounter situations of the sort Daniel describes. Although the canvas is a large one, it is not out of reach. This much is recognised even by those who hold that Daniel (and chapter 11 in particular) was written around the time of Antiochus Epiphanes to give the Jews hope in a hopeless situation. They note that the sequence will build confidence on the part of the listeners and that, even as the details converge around the reality they are experiencing, God can still be expected to act in deliverance. For those early readers, perhaps, there was even room for a spectacular intervention in the cataclysmic finale that the framework itself predicts. For Christians throughout the ages, a similar prospect holds good.

And the book of Daniel is always trying to embrace these two perspectives – the broad pattern of God interacting with nations and the microscopic perspective of God's interaction with individuals to bring good out of difficult times. Daniel's own experience reflects this as God looks after the vulnerable exiles and also as he engages with Nebuchadnezzar and the royal court. The stories and the visions both share this dual interest in God working on a large scale and also on a small scale. They are both of a piece.

A type of vision

And surely these are exactly the sorts of visions we would expect someone like Daniel to have. The strategist who has worked at the heart of the biggest empire in the world would naturally be able to take in plans that stretch generations ahead. The civil servant who needs to know that it will all work out, may be expected to take an interest in the details. The administrator who has run sections of the machinery of government might be expected to take an interest in the evolving shape of national borders and in military commanders whose campaigns move so quickly, they hardly seem to touch the ground. Daniel, the people-person with an ability to make friends and make friendships work, would have had a great interest in the world of people. The way in which Daniel's vision stretches ahead and spreads out, closely mirrors the sort of view he might have been expected to take in his work in the royal court.

In a sense, Daniel's spiritual ministry and his secular experience have much in common – they are all of a piece. This becomes clearer if we take a look at Ezekiel. In his first chapter, Ezekiel the priest is standing by the Kebar River, just down the road from Babylon, I understand, near Nippur. Now what is the great theme of Ezekiel's visions? The bright thread running through Ezekiel is the glory of God (e.g. Ezek 1:4-28; 8:2-4; 9:3). As a priest, Ezekiel is into the temple, the house of God and the relationship between the glory of God and the house of God. Ezekiel must look on as the glory departs (Ezek 10:4-19) and eventually, sees it returning (Ezek 43:2-5) to fill the temple once more. Even geography is about glory for Ezekiel: 'I will display my glory among the nations, and all the nations will see the punishment I inflict and the hand I lay upon them' (Ezek 39:21).

I read the write-up of the reality TV series, *Beauty and the Geek*, which was sensitive and positive, but I did not actually get around to watching it. Apparently, it was based around teaming inept but highly intelligent young men with beautiful young women to undertake a series of missions, and it signalled the way in which a term of abuse is being rehabilitated. It is not hard to see why. The software and internet revolutions have propelled a generation of nerds into a range of socially accept-able roles, notably those of millionaire, multi-millionaire, and billionaire. And all credit to them! Our society is more indebted than we realise to insular geniuses, and it is nice to see some of them getting a bit of recognition.

Geeks and anoraks neglect the social conventions of their day to focus on the one great love of their lives – be it trains, litera-ture, coding syntax, art, or whatever. Their ability to be entirely taken up with a single topic provides them with a limitless source of mysterious happiness. Occasionally, we come to recognise the importance of the goal to which they have devot-ed their lives, and they enjoy a spell of popularity, too. Often we never come to share their passion, and they lie neglected.

However, the idea that we have room for just one great love in our lives is a theme that Jesus repeatedly promotes. The Pearl Merchant (Matt 13:45,46), for instance, jettisons everything else in his life in order to possess the pearl he really wants. Jesus' teaching on money is also couched in terms of competing loves (e.g. Matt 6:24). Where this unfashionable focus leads to sur-prising behaviour, Jesus is quick to commend where others would ignore or condemn – for instance, the woman with the alabaster jar (e.g. Matt 26:6-13), Mary with her perfume (John 12:3-8), or the widow offering her last coins at the Temple (Luke 21:1-4). This relentless pursuit of the one great love is clearly dif-ficult for us at times (Matt 19:27): 'Peter answered him, "We have left everything to follow you! What then will there be for us?"'

I am a bit of an anorak myself. When the lottery numbers come up, I end up trying to work out whether fewer or more than one in three is a prime number. These days, even my wife will pass some remark on the number of primes in the sequence. I am very much afraid that there will soon be other voices on the sofa commenting on the randomness of the winning combination, as the next generation of Youngs comes through. Perhaps it is not surprising, then, that I am encouraged to discover that God seems to be looking for a bit of the geek in each of us. And I am glad to see that these terms are being recovered for better use.

So, what sort of person is Ezekiel, and what is the impact of his visions? For me, Ezekiel is a bit of an anorak. He isn't into primes but he is wild about measurement. In his acted-out demonstrations for the people, he is always counting off days, measuring out his meals – grain and water – precisely and compulsively (Ezek 4:4-14). He gets even more excited when let loose with his measuring line to sort out a spot for the temple in Jerusalem and space for the Levites who will look after it (Ezek 45:1-6). Even his concept of justice (not uniquely his, of course) is anchored around accurate measures of volume and currency, so that people will not be ripped off (Ezek 45:10-12).

Now, would Ezekiel have been able to foresee the rise and fall of nations, the thrust of this ruler or the collapse of that administration? I don't think so. As far as I can see, Ezekiel is not that interested in organisations. I doubt if he would have understood that type of vision enough to pass it on, even if he had seen it. Ezekiel's colossal contribution lies in the great love of his life. Ezekiel brings us the glory of God. It is the one thing that really satisfies him. And the impact that Ezekiel makes is the moral imperative – a call to worship beneath the blazing glory of the God he worships. There is something of the glory geek about Ezekiel. He does not try to talk people around. It may be that he is incapable of persuasion. But the vision he presents of a blindingly holy God is compelling. It exposed the double dealers of his day. It speaks to us today.

Against this, we have Daniel with his easy style and ready way with people. He can take in situations at a glance, slow down the pace of disaster and find the steadying word that gives him time to pray and find the answer. Daniel is a practical person who finds practical ways to deal with the gritty reality of life. He can also take in a big picture and grasp the practical complexities behind it.

Both men are committed to living a highly moral life before God. However, Daniel's appeal lies largely in his track record in the service of kings. Ezekiel's appeal lies in the moral force of a life consumed by serving God.

And as you look around, you will see both types of visionary. So long as the vision is backed by the life, both types of vision can be valid. Down through the years there have been many Christian leaders whose authority has stemmed from a moral drive and personal holiness. They are not always practical people and rarely care much for what people think of them. General Booth, founder of the Salvation Army, was one of the few evangelical Christians who made much of an impression on Rudyard Kipling. The General said he would stand on his head and play the trombone with his toes if he thought it would bring anyone to Christ. That degree of focus and dedication meant something to the writer who saw so much hypocrisy and guile in his world. A bit outlandish and unconventional, but the drive has had a lasting impact.

There was once a class of missionary who had something of Ezekiel's unworldly fanaticism. Henry Martyn and Adoniram Judson are not that well known today but their focus and drive led to great achievements to the glory of God, particularly in translating the scriptures – Martyn into Arabic and Judson into what was then Burmese. I guess both would have been viewed as gifted geeks these days, and both paid an extreme personal price for their dedication as did those around them. Judson lost two wives and Martyn never got around to marrying, although it seems there was someone he wanted to marry. Incidentally, Ezekiel pays a heavy price when his wife dies (Ezek 24:15-18). A more recent example (though without the geekiness) might be John Stott, whose dedication, moral rectitude and scholarship has been a quiet support to millions of Christians over the past few decades.

More practical visionaries also abound. A recent example concerned some friends from a church I used to attend some way away, now. Somehow, they got into visiting Romania and put together several practical teams to help out. The teams were culled from independent churches and some of the people had worked together in the past. They represented a good mix of practical skills – builders, carpenters, bodywork specialists and mechanics, managers in commerce, and eventually a plumber. Their first job was to renovate an orphanage, but in time they got a vision for something that would last longer and serve the local church.

They hit on the idea of building a bakery – partly to meet the immediate need for food, but also to provide employment and income for a needy community. The bakery vision took a long time to fulfil, but the team set up a charity, raised tens of thousands of pounds (mainly, I suspect, through personal giving), forged links with local Christians in Romania, bought the land and built the premises. It lay vacant for a year while they waited for the gas to be connected, but the last I heard, it was baking bread. Today, with travel so cheap and the rest of the world so accessible, this type of vision is valid and readily fulfilled. You may well know of Christian groups engaged in very practical ministries from your local church.

On the other hand, there are visions where the match is missing. I remember being put in charge of the midweek meeting at church. I had a vision to build numbers from the twenty or so to over forty. It did not happen despite my best endeavours. I stated my goal, I worked hard to bring in speakers with something to say, we had videos, we had thematic series, but numbers didn't rise. I encouraged people to come along, but we never crept close to the target for anything other than the occasional, one-off event. In retrospect, my guess is that building up numbers at a church service requires that overwhelming moral authority – which isn't really my gift. A better solution came through home groups, which, alongside the midweek meeting, now provide some weeknight support and fellowship for about half the membership.

Today, there are lots of people with a vision for others. Some are explicit in stating that God has something to say. Some will phrase things differently, but they are still setting an agenda for others to go after. Most of the time, our discussion centres upon whether we believe God speaks through people in this way or that way. I would like to defocus from that issue. I suspect that part of the debate centres around the way in which different traditions articulate their visions. I want to steer away from the question of how you believe God reveals his will to people today, partly because it is a really difficult question and partly because I think there are some other questions that are worth considering in the context of Daniel and Ezekiel. In any case, I suspect Christians change their views on visions very slowly and not usually through reading books.

So let's return to the question of evaluating such visions and see what Daniel has to offer. Does the vision match the experience and skills of the visionary? If it does, it is worth pressing forward in the evaluation. Specifically, Daniel and the cross references to Ezekiel indicate to me that there are at least two kinds of vision – the essentially practical vision and the vision that is essentially oriented to God's glory amongst his people. There may well be others. We will return to this before the end of the chapter, but there are also some questions at the end that may help you to grapple with this key point – how does the vision go with the visionary and is there a match?

This will hurt me more than it hurts you

However, Daniel also provides us with another test for the evaluation of visionaries. We have not used Nebuchadnezzar's second dream (Dan 4:10-18) in this section because it is a very personal sort of vision. However, once Daniel realises that this dream foretells a terrible judgement upon the king, his reaction is telling: 'My lord, if only the dream applied to your enemies and its meaning to your adversaries' (Dan 4:19). We have noted Daniel's people skills. Daniel really loves people. His friendships cost him something and he cannot deliver painful messages except at great personal cost.

Let us compare Daniel's reaction here to Jonah's. Jonah is another prophet sent with a message of judgement to a superpower of the day. The denizens of Nineveh (Jonah 1:2) are Jonah's target audience. The trouble with Jonah is that he wants the judgement to fall. He hates these people and he is glad that God is going to do something about them. From what I understand, he had some justification for loathing a people whose arrogant and cruel armies had been so successful.

His main problem lies in suspecting that God will show mercy in the end. We have an early example of prophet-rage when he is deprived at the finish of a grandstand view of falling judgement on all those awful people (Jonah 4:1-5). The judgement does not fall because Jonah and his God are committed to very different outcomes.

In both cases, the message is one of judgement, but the big difference lies in the messenger. Clearly, in both cases the message is authentic, but in Jonah's case there is something wrong with the messenger. In fact, the whole book of Jonah is shot through with the ambiguity of the unsuitable messenger. He is unwilling to take the message in the first place and he is angry as well as disappointed when his audience listens and repents. The book of Jonah reaches one of the most unsatisfactory conclusions in the canon, just an ongoing argument between the prophet and his God. The balance between the good of the city and the prophet's personal comfort remains deliciously unresolved. In fact, the book has the air of a modern novel at the end.

Clearly, the attitude of the prophet is not a clear guide as to the validity of the vision – Jonah is highly unsatisfactory as a prophet (although the fact that he can tell us about his struggle indicates that he moves on in his attitude). Nevertheless, I worry at times about the number of angry prophets we seem to hear – people who seem to delight in the fact that they have some bad news for us all.

An incident from twenty years ago springs to mind. A chap showed up at the Christian Union one evening and announced that he had a message from God for the students. He did not want to tell the executive committee what this message was – in fact he made it quite clear he did not have any time for executive committees. He was a man on a mission and it was up to everyone else to sit up and listen. Clearly this was a very tricky one to call. Were we meeting an Ezekiel, with that strong moral dynamic to his life, to whom we simply had to listen? Or was this a would-be Jonah, high on attitude? The decision we reached was that if he could not discuss the message with the leadership, the leadership would hardly be taking a responsible approach in letting an unknown messenger with an unknown message loose on the Christian Union that evening.

I guess the fact that I can remember the encounter now indicates something of the turbulent feelings I experienced as we left the chap. On the one hand, there was a sense of relief. I was pretty sure that the message would be a harsh one. On the other hand, there was that sense of worry that God might have had something to say in spite of the unpalatable situation. Looking back, I feel comfortable that we made a sound decision, and I hope we would make the same decision again.

The angry prophet has been around for some time. It is much easier to get the anger than to get the vision. A year or two ago, I tried to piece together the passages in Proverbs that related to the fool, one of those characters who appear throughout the collection. I noted how many times the fool is an angry man:

> A fool shows his annoyance at once, but a prudent man overlooks an insult (Prov 12:16).

> A wise man fears the LORD and shuns evil, but a fool is hotheaded and reckless (Prov 14:16).

> A quick-tempered man does foolish things, and a crafty man is hated (Prov 14:17).

> It is to a man's honour to avoid strife, but every fool is quick to quarrel (Prov 20:3).

> Stone is heavy and sand a burden, but provocation by a fool is heavier than both (Prov 27:3).

> If a wise man goes to court with a fool, the fool rages and scoffs, and there is no peace (Prov 29:9).

> A fool gives full vent to his anger, but a wise man keeps himself under control (Prov 29:11).

So much is achieved today by angry visionaries, impatient with the present, unwilling to dwell any longer with the stupidities of inflexible systems. It seems natural that the church should follow suit, especially since it has a tradition, at least on superficial inspection, of angry prophets. James is, as usual, very blunt: 'for man's anger does not bring about the righteous life that God desires' (Jas 1:20).

So, it seems to me that Daniel's attitude is helpful, if not in authenticating the message itself, at least in indicating the suitability of the messenger in bringing it. And I have noticed that my own perspective has changed: I used to listen carefully to the content of what people brought before the church – increasingly I find myself wondering how much they are enjoying it. What sort of attitude does the vision-bearer have? The New Testament is full of warnings against dodgy teachers with intricate theological propositions and people who enjoy the limelight just a little too much (e.g. Col 2:16-19; 1 Tim 1:3-7; 3 John 9).

A few years ago, I picked up a book on reverence. Before long, I found it hard to escape a feeling that the writer rather enjoyed the exercise of humbling congregations before God. I left the book unfinished. Perhaps I was uncomfortably challenged by the content. Perhaps the writer was better on the platform than in print. Perhaps he was better at his ministry than he was at discussing it. But life is too short to finish every book you start, especially if you have grown uneasy with the writer.

These days, when I find myself feeling uncomfortable with the delivery, I try to face up to this rather than, as I once did, trying to distance myself from the feelings and concentrating my efforts on viewing the content objectively. And I think there is some scriptural support for examining the motivation and attitude of the prophet, as well as considering the vision. Often, I discover that there is something of concern about the angry prophet.

In my late teens and early twenties I had several good friends who attended a house fellowship not that far away. Looking back, I can see that an examination of the attitude of the leadership would have provided an early amber light on the vision as a whole. There were leaders who were quite sure they could get God's message and deliver it uncompromisingly. Several people are still a little scarred.

Does this mean that messages of judgement are out? Not at all. No-one spoke with greater conviction than Jesus about the holiness of God and the inevitable impact of its collision in wrath upon unrepentant humanity. But the key word is humanity. Can't you catch the humanity here? 'O Jerusalem, Jerusalem, you who kill the prophets and stone those sent to you, how often I have longed to gather your children together, as a hen gathers her chicks under her wings, but you were not willing. Look, your house is left to you desolate' (Matt 23:37,38).

Strategy for today

Clearly we need vision today. 'Where there is no revelation, the people cast off restraint' (Prov 29:18). I once heard a story about a Christian driving instructor who had a verse for every piece of advice. His verse for the rear-view mirror was the Authorised Version of this verse – 'Without a vision, the people perish'.

So how can we apply it today? Well, here are three types of vision to be approached with caution. The first is the practical vision brought by the unworldly, often spiritual soul. It can work, particularly in building projects where there are professionals, such as architects and engineers, to moderate the vision. But beware before you buy it. Second, there is the strong moral directive, delivered by a person whose life will not bear the same scrutiny as he or she wants to apply to everyone else. Such people may have practical insights, but on the spiritual front, care is needed. Finally, beware the angry prophet, or the visionary who seems to take pleasure in condemning the rest.

On the other hand, where the thoroughly godly man or woman has a challenge to bring, it will be worth meditating on, however unpalatable it seems at first sight. Likewise, practical visions, especially when backed by appropriate experience and insight, can be a great blessing in building up many aspects of the church's ministry. And, of course, even the hardest challenge can be acceptable if delivered with compassion and humility.

It seems to me that the trick is to find a vision for our churches, missions or other Christian initiatives that embrace both the spiritual and the practical. We need Daniels and Ezekiels. The difficulty, of course, is that people with one set of gifts are not always drawn to those who have the other. To the visionary with the moral imperatives, the practical vision is beside the point. It may even admit of shades of grey that are totally unacceptable to the absolutist. How long, I wonder, might Ezekiel have survived in Daniel's shoes? On the other hand the practical visionary may find the intensity of the moral vision difficult to manage all the time. He or she may also find that it ignores very difficult practical problems.

This, then, is the great opportunity for peacemakers – integrating the contributions of people whose approaches are so disparate that they seem to conflict, and helping each to see his or her role alongside the other. And now, I think I have gone about as far as I can go. The practicalities of identifying your Daniels and your Ezekiels and finding how to amalgamate their respective contributions into an effective strategy, these are things to be worked out by you and your leadership teams.

Thinking it through

1. How do your friends try to find out or guess at the future? Pick three approaches and discuss them from a Christian perspective.

2. Track the number four through Daniel and Revelation. What do you think the number meant to the early readers?

3. Towards the end of a service, a lady comes up to the vicar and says she has a picture she wants to share with the

congregation. The vicar has just a short time to make an initial response. Laying aside any prejudices you may have for or against this approach, and considering the material in this chapter – what would you say are the key issues on which the vicar might base a response?

4. A journalist in your church wants to produce a news-sheet for distribution around the estate on which your church is sited. What factors would help you steer the discussion when you meet to discuss the proposal.

5. The young people and their leaders come forward with an idea to build a library annex to a school in Kenya, with which your church has connections. How would you explore their vision with them and what preparatory work might you ask them to complete before you meet with them again?

6. How would you classify Nehemiah's vision? How did it stack up with his experience and skills?

7. Think of one practical visionary you know and one moral visionary. In what ways does each wind the other up? To what extent are their contributions complementary?

8. Your church is planning to produce a strategy and you have been asked to present a set of headings at the next leadership meeting. What topics do you think should be covered by such a document? How would you find the people to write those sections?

9. How important is consensus to vision? Why?

10. Your pastor wants to extend the auditorium of your church to treble the seating capacity. How might you explore this vision? What alternatives might you ask some members of your leadership team to flesh out?

11. Why do companies and churches produce new strategies so frequently?

12. Thomas Edison said that inspiration is 98% perspiration. How true is that in church?

6

Interpreting the visions

What are the difficulties in making sense of the visions? First, there is the question of whether we have real prophecy here, written before it happened, or whether the prophetic element is a literary device, written retrospectively. Certainly a retrospective review, with its recurring image of failing kingdoms would serve as a helpful backdrop to the dire straits being experienced by God's people when they first encountered the text. On this reading, it should be possible to decode the dreams, symbol by symbol and identify each of the characters mentioned. We might expect the historian to exercise some judgement in terms of the emphasis given to each historical character, but would anticipate what was essentially a complete description.

If, on the other hand this is a glimpse of the future through prophetic eyes, we may accept a more stylised approach. One might find it more difficult to pull everything together in terms of historical fact, in much the same way as one cannot identify each hair in Van Gogh's beard through his brush strokes. The impressionist's self portraits are very telling (and well worth having, should you discover a spare copy in your grandmother's attic), but they do not equate to reality in that one-to-one sense. In fact, Van Gogh's use of colour and the way he strokes in those unexpected shades are evidence of genius rather than ignorance. We might expect the prophetic view to be a bit more like an impressionist's view of the world – brightly coloured and highly exciting, while retaining an essence of what it portrays.

Whichever way you look at it, you will have to get to grips with a lot of history – and that is not my domain. From my limited reading the period looks a fun one to study – but I could not possibly approach Daniel credibly or helpfully in print from that perspective. You need a good commentary for that and will probably have to widen your reading further to make entertaining progress. If you get the bug to study further from reading this – great! As I have always said, I tend to take Daniel at face value and the easiest reading is that this government official saw visions related to the future. On that basis, I am happy to run with the text as prophecy.

Another hot potato concerns the end times. Jesus said he would return to earth a second time – for instance, during his lengthy discussion with the disciples that is recorded in Matthew chapters 24 and 25. That passage refers explicitly back to Daniel (Matt 24:15), and indicates that, for Jesus, the vision still had something for the future. A return by Jesus is attested by the angels at the ascension (Acts 1:11) and was passed on by the apostles as part of the earliest Christian doctrine (e.g. 1 Thess 4:16; 2 Pet 3:3-13). Finally, the book of Revelation is full of material not dissimilar to Daniel's visions – scene after scene of wild and colourful takes on events that lead up to the end of all time. It is interesting how many church Bible studies try to break off the first three chapters of Revelation (which appear tractable) from the remaining 19 (which look a bit tricky), in much the same way as we like to split Daniel in two. Nevertheless, the 'seventy sevens' (Dan 9:24-27) has soaked up enormous amounts of scholarship over the years and I am not in a position to contribute new insights from that perspective.

My fundamental belief is that the Bible has been given to us to support us in our faith. While I believe there will be passages sufficiently mysterious, obscure, or just plain rewarding to be worth a lifetime of study, I cannot believe that Scripture yields its greatest rewards only to the greatest intellects. In fact, there is evidence that Jesus saw the balance sliding the other way: 'At that time Jesus said, "I praise you, Father, Lord of heaven and earth, because you have hidden these things from the wise and learned, and revealed them to little children. Yes, Father, for this was your good pleasure"' (Matt 11:25,26).

I am keen that Christians familiarise themselves with the prophets, but I do not buy the argument that you need a PhD in inter-testamental world history to be blessed in working through Daniel's visions. Again, I believe Christians need to understand about Jesus' return but I don't see that complete familiarity with the various viewpoints – and with the trickier elements of Daniel, in particular – is a prerequisite to grasping the doctrine soundly.

What I really want to find is a way into the book that does not rely too heavily on knowing lots of things. I guess I am also keen to see the agenda set around things that are meaningful to the average Christian today, rather than around the divisions of the past. So here are a few approaches that attempt to cut the cake a little differently.

A pattern repeated

Looking at the very coarsest patterns in Daniel, part of the good news is that even despots have a limited shelf-life. There is no message in Daniel, as far as I can see, that indicates that bad rulers will be replaced by better rulers. In many ways, Nebuchadnezzar, with his close encounters with God and evangelistic edicts, is the best of the bunch. But it is not downhill all the way from there. Sure, the dismissive and arrogant Belshazzar has his turn at the top, but then Cyrus comes along with a decree that allows the Jews home to rebuild the temple.

The first message of this approach to Daniel, then, is that kings and rulers have their allotted time. The new king may view God-fearers with greater or lesser tolerance. On the whole, Daniel finds that rulers respond positively to hardworking exiles who will work loyally for the monarch. But he sees harsh clashes ahead. In the meantime, Daniel's example is to work hard and well for the good of the kingdom. Paul's approach under the Caesars is much the same – Christians should pray for the freedom to worship. 'I urge, then, first of all, that requests, prayers, intercession and thanksgiving be made for everyone – for kings and all those in authority, that we may live peaceful and quiet lives in all godliness and holiness' (1 Tim 2:1,2). And there can be some surprises. Saddam Hussein appears to have allowed Christians in Iraq some freedom in worship, although his regime was characterised by a great deal of brutality. As we look around today, there are strict governments under which the church is doing pretty well, while some moderate states are giving Christians a tough time.

But is that the limit of the good news in Daniel – that bad regimes will not last forever, or that many regimes will take a tolerant line on personal worship? The fact remains that a bad regime in the full bloom of its power can spill a lot of innocent blood. And it does not have to go that far for the godly to feel threatened. Whoever wrote the book of Hebrews notes that we are all vulnerable well below the shadow of martyrdom – 'Let us fix our eyes on Jesus, the author and perfecter of our faith, who for the joy set before him endured the cross, scorning its shame, and sat down at the right hand of the throne of God. Consider him who endured such opposition from sinful men, so that you will not grow weary and lose heart. In your struggle against sin, you have not yet resisted to the point of shedding your blood' (Heb 12:2-4).

The fact that regime-change comes in the end may be of limited comfort if you do not last that long. Daniel does not hold out the promise that everyone will survive the purges. But there are other encouragements in Daniel's view of the future that will help those going through the mill under a tyrant whose power, for the present, is awesome and whose intent is hostile.

To begin with, the whole book of Daniel challenges the view that a tyrant's power is ever absolute. In his own experience, Daniel sees that God has a way of getting through, even to tyrants. God has ways of achieving regime-changes that do not necessarily involve changing the monarch, although if that is what it takes, that too is an option. For thirty years or more under Nebuchadnezzar, Daniel has personal experience of God at work, changing, modifying, sometimes crunching with eye-watering ferocity against, the regime of the day. Later, in his dreams, the same message rings out as he sees happenings, in a heavenly realm, that run alongside and sometimes ahead of the strutting tyrant on earth.

So, in Daniel's world of waking and dreaming, God does not leave himself powerless, even before powerful people. If, as Shadrach, Meshach and Abednego observe, their God chooses not to save them, it is because he chooses not to do so, not because he cannot do so (Dan 3:16-18).

Local and global

In both the stories and the visions, there are several scales at which God is active. God works on behalf of a few exiles, but is also active at top level with Nebuchadnezzar and his strategic plans for the nation. God is the God of vulnerable individuals and the God over empires. The interesting piece is how these different levels connect together in the book. We will consider a couple of them here.

Throughout the visions, the closing focus, particularly

towards the end, reminds us that this is not just a book about global strategy nor about the individuals caught up in it all – there are other layers and subtleties of plot in which Daniel knows God to be active. In Daniel's own life, he knows he is living through the times of the head of gold in Nebuchadnezzar's dream. Despite the huge cogs that are grinding together, Daniel is also aware of God's hand in his own life. The dreams, which focus on different scales, show that God does not have to take his eye off the global ball to be aware of, and interested in, life on smaller scales. The first way in which these levels connect together – from the largest scale directly to the most personal scale – is through the individuals involved – sometimes incidentally, almost as spectators, sometimes as influential figures, such as Daniel and his friends. At one level, Daniel is a record of God's protection in scary times.

I guess we don't often get to be a close-in spectator in auspicious times. The nearest I have come to being a small observer while the cogs of history are changing gear was as a child during the Six Day War. We had gone to spend the summer of '67 in the hills just outside of Beirut, partly as a vacation, and partly to try to get something done about the artificial legs I was rapidly outgrowing. The visit to the hospital had drawn a bit of a blank, but the holiday was going well in one of the most beautiful places on earth. My Dad had recently arrived on holiday, having stayed in the Gulf later than the rest of the family to continue his work, but the commencement of hostilities meant airlifting all Americans out. My Mom is an American, so we made a night journey down into Beirut with another family, packed into the only transport available, a VW Beetle. I don't recall being at all afraid and can still recall acts of personal kindness and protection – the family who had stocked up for the long wait and shared a breakfast with us, the armed guards on the coach to the airport the next morning, the Boeing 707 that took us to Turkey.

After an uncertain couple of days, we ended up in London, and for me, it meant getting a completely new set of legs at Roehampton. Personal protection, personal blessing in hazardous times. I don't know if that makes much sense as a story to you, but it is my only experience of being part of something really global, and yet seeing some very difficult personal barriers overcome at the same time. It is one of the few times when I have seen the very large and the very small scale, side by side.

You may be old enough to have seen the downfall of a super-power. Apart from its political and economic aims (which you may endorse or abhor), the communist system set its stall against faith in God, and for many Christians, this meant decades of hardship behind the Iron Curtain. I grew up in a world in which the steady progress of communism across the globe seemed inexorable. For years it looked like the transition to a communist state was a one-way ticket. Yet, in a surprising turn of events, it was the communist leaders in Eastern Europe who went down like dominoes, for some, the end coming bru-tally at the hands of their own people.

But how does God fit into all this? Well, what sort of an answer are we looking for? If we want to decode history in a sort of goodies-against-baddies way, I am not sure Daniel has anything to offer. If we never see beyond the political realities, the book is essential mute. But I think there is something more here about the large scale and the small scale. It is not just that Daniel sees God's hand in the minutiae in the middle of upheaval, he is also looking at these small things in a different way, and assigns them a priority quite different from the priori-ties that other viewers – perhaps even ourselves – would have chosen.

A leaflet has sculled around my files for years now, called, *The story of Zia Nodrat*. Despite many purges on paperwork, I have never felt able to throw it out, although I am not really sure what to make of the story. It certainly has a flavour of Daniel about it – a government that takes a dim view of Christians, two superpowers, and an individual caught up in it all. According to my leaflet, Zia Nodrat was a blind teenage Afghan in the '60s who became a Christian through listening to Voice of the Gospel broadcasts out of Ethiopia. During the early '70s, he was a prominent member of the small Christian community in Kabul and the event that sticks with me concerns the church building itself.

Apparently, back in 1959, President Eisenhower had request-ed that a church be built in Kabul for foreign diplomats and local Christians as part of a reciprocal arrangement that had seen a mosque erected in Washington DC. Just over a decade later, the cornerstone was laid. Apparently, a few years later, the authorities decided to bulldoze the building. According to this source, the destruction was completed on 17 July 1973. That night the monarchy fell and Afghanistan became a republic. A few years later, there was a coup and most people will remember the Russian invasion a year or so after that, in 1979.

It is the interplay of the very small scale against the larger scale global politics that intrigues me about the story. Was the timing a coincidence? I really don't know. I only recall vaguely that at the time, your average Western Christian was probably more interested in the superpower balance than the future of a small Christian community or the fate of its place of worship.

So how would Daniel have narrated this passage of history? At the time, it would have been difficult to maintain that the use of looted tableware from the Jewish temple was a significant element at Belshazzar's final feast. The wildness, the colour, the personalities, the physical sense of fear, even, these might have been what the professional historian would have watched and recorded. And yet Daniel sees things differently, because he has decided to watch differently.

And at times the writers of Scripture will take a view so contrary that it takes our breath away. As I write, the women's marathon is underway at the Olympics in Athens and it reminds me of one of the most stunning clashes between another writer – Luke – and the prevailing view. In Acts 17:21, Luke feels compelled to add a cultural footnote, which he does in brackets. '(All the Athenians and the foreigners who lived there spent their time doing nothing but talking about and listening to the latest ideas.)'

All the glory, philosophy, tradition and history, glossed over in a single bracket! And while Daniel is much more engaged in the local culture, he is still able to bring a very different perspective to bear. Surprising things are happening, once you know what you are looking for.

Even the story of the Eastern Bloc dictators has the occasional unexpected twist that puts the small scale next to the global. There was a story on the radio recently about Erich Honecker, the East German dictator whose demise followed the fall of the Berlin Wall. Interested, I picked up some other details from the web in a published sermon preached on 9 July 2000 by a Dr Amerson. Destitute and facing charges of treason, it was a Christian pastor, Uwe Homer, and his wife who took the Honeckers in. I cannot imagine that pastors in East Germany needed any more grief in their despised and impoverished existence, but this family rose to the challenge to show God's love to someone who had headed a system that aimed to suppress any awareness of God's love. Their compassion is all the more amazing, since their church membership had barred the way to a university education for their own children. God is as capable of closing with the powerful now as he ever has been.

So three messages run through the stories and the visions, whatever experience or scale of the future is under the microscope. First, kings and kingdoms come to an end and God is committed to judging each individual and situation in the end. Throughout such regimes, Daniel brings encouragement to the individual that God is able to protect and support them through difficult times. Other parts of Scripture remind us that those who trust in God are not immune to trouble, but the message from Daniel is essentially one of comfort.

Second, Daniel reminds us that no matter how impervious that regime appears to be to outside influences, God is able to intervene. Sometimes he intervenes to the destruction of that regime, sometimes to change its outlook without wrecking it. Finally, if you know how to look and where to look, you might discover that God is already intervening in surprising and unexpected ways that not everyone will notice, perhaps at the personal, or small scale level.

But I think we can go a little further in connecting up these different scales or levels, because the pattern of rising and falling despots seems to repeat itself at each level. There are a number or ways in which we might illustrate this. A musician might allude to a haunting theme that flits in and out of a piece of music. An artist might prefer a pattern or set of colours that recur in a painting, or throughout a set of paintings. I like the idea of a fractal.

The future as a fractal

Fractals are one of the beautiful by-products of chaos theory. Many of us will have encountered them as those fabulous abstract pictures with intricate details. The thing about a fractal is the way in which certain features are preserved, no matter what the scale. You look at the big picture, and you see a pattern. You magnify it and look at a small section and the same features are there. You magnify further and the same pattern emerges again. In fact, because fractals are mathematical creations, you can go on scaling up for ever and you will be faced with the same sort of pattern every time you look.

Fractals provide a great way to describe things in real life that elude a more conventional mathematical description. For instance, it is possible to build a fractal representation of a tree relatively easily because the way in which the trunk splits into the main branches is rather like the way in which those in turn branch out and the way in which twigs split into twiglets. Fractals, then, can be used to build nice models of trees, coastlines, rivers, and other natural systems. One of my favourite science writers is a chap called James Gleick, and his book, *Chaos*, provides a well-written, well-illustrated way into the subject. But how does that help us here?

It seems to me that at whatever scale we view Daniel's world, the picture is very much the same. Kings rise and fall. New kings take their place. Whether the timescale is centuries (as in Nebuchadnezzar's dream and Daniel's first dream) or decades, perhaps even down to a few years (as in some of the events in chapter 11), the pattern is very similar. Empires come, empires go. Kings come, kings go. Rulers wax and wane. Second, the people who rise to power appear all-powerful while they are there. Once in position, it appears that they can do as they please. Only a fool would remind an absolute monarch that his predecessor is now dead and that he, too, will pass on. While he is in power, his power over his world appears absolute.

So how does this fractal approach help us today? Well, it helps me to remember that the pattern in a fractal remains the same whatever the magnification and wherever you look. So if we wind the clock forward and turn up the magnification until it is our own world in view, we probably get the same pattern. Simply cranking the clock forward to the present time does not change the basic pattern. Cranking up the magnification makes it no less true. By clocking forward and magnifying up, sooner or later we can see ourselves, or our friends, under the microscope. It may not be a government regime that applies most pressure to our work, our ethics, or our Christian witness. It may be a smaller dictator – a local politician, the CEO of our company, perhaps even our boss. The restless sea is always churning up new leaders – some of them good, some of them otherwise.

During my time in industry, it was evident that the life expectancy of senior management was brief – often less than two years. A new leader would be appointed and issue the new agenda as though it were being set for decades to come. For a while the new agenda would push all else aside and then, overnight, there would be a new hand at the helm. Although the cycle was transparently obvious from outside, it had a powerful grip on those inside the system, introducing huge uncertainties, extra work, and perhaps a harsh environment for a while.

I do not know what your situation is. I have no idea what inflexible system you may feel you suffer under. I cannot imagine who the person is who seems to hold the key to your future in his or her hand. But the message of Daniel is not to be fooled by appearance. You can work with confidence under this person. You can pray for this person and ask God to bring you to a position where you actually want the best for this person. And you can trust God to intervene, as appropriate.

I know that is easy for me to say. I appreciate how many times I have resented situations that were beyond my control. But the history as a fractal approach to Daniel encourages me to turn the clock forwards and turn up the magnification until it is my situation that is under the microscope. And once I see myself there, I can expect Daniel's God to still be God over my situation. I can expect him to bring the situation to a conclusion in due time. I can expect God to intervene – but on his terms, not mine. And I can expect him to deal with the loose ends of the situation – again, on his terms and to his timescale, not mine.

Another way in – something big is happening

Another approach to Daniel is to stand back and see what actually happened and follow it up to the present day. Let's begin, then, by asking, what actually was happening during 'the time of those kings' (Dan 2:44)? Most of us assume that nothing happened until Jesus came, died, rose again, ascended and commissioned his followers to take the good news to the ends of the earth. The taking of the message to the ends of the earth (Acts 1:8) corresponds to the rock that becomes a mountain and fills the earth. And if we look at it that way, the expansive action happens once the Gospels are over. On this view, the missionary movement starts in Acts. I think there is something to be said for seeking a start with the exile.

The exile was not just an exercise in transplanting a group of the more educated Jews to Babylon and allowing them home after seventy years. As I understand it, the exile triggered the setting up of Jewish communities all over the known world. It did not take long for Jews in these expatriate communities to outnumber those back at home – even after the return. As we read through Acts, we discover that it was these communities to whom Paul and his companions first took the gospel message. It would be hard to overstate the importance of the build-up of these communities around the world in terms of providing a network through which the church would spread its message.

A second important development that began with the exile and that continued as an 'inward investment' with the returning exiles, was the synagogue. Clearly, with the temple destroyed and the Jews separated even from the site on which it had stood, there was a need to find a way of worshipping God without a temple. The vacuum was filled by the synagogue, with its emphasis on Scripture.

Again, I have to stress that this isn't my specialist subject, but it seems that wherever Jewish communities settled around the world, their early priority was to establish a synagogue. So successful was this approach that synagogues were established back in the homeland, and even when temple worship was possible once more, the synagogue still provided the weekly context in which most Jews worshipped and learnt the Scriptures. Certainly, Jesus taught in the synagogue at Capernaum (Mark 1:21) and Nazareth (Luke 4:16). Some notable healings took place in synagogues (Mark 3:1; Luke 4:33-37; 13:10-16) and Jesus performed at least one great miracle in restoring to life the daughter of a synagogue ruler (Mark 5:22-43) as well as healing the servant of a centurion who had sponsored the building of a synagogue (Luke 7:2-10).

These communities around the world needed access to their Scriptures in a language they could read and, as time went on, Greek became that unifying language. Skirting around all kinds of tricky questions about the canon and the role of the scribes in pulling it all together, it was the expatriate Jewish community in Egypt that produced the Scriptures in Greek – the Septuagint. It was this translation that the New Testament writers quote in their own writings and it had a profound impact in providing a common revelation of God's word to Jews across the known world.

These three developments – Jewish communities around the world, the synagogues and the Scriptures in Greek that went with them – were critical to the successful spread of the gospel message. Like his master before him, Paul's first port of call for worship was the local synagogue – be it Athens (Acts 17:17), Berea (Acts 17:10), Corinth (Acts 18:1-4), Ephesus (Acts 18:19), Iconium (Acts 14:1), Pisidian Antioch (Acts 13:14) or Thessalonica (Acts 17:1,2).

These communities provided a speedy communication system for developments in Jewish thinking, something which is illustrated by Paul's discovery of a dozen worshippers who had been baptised into the tradition of John the Baptist (Acts 19:1-7). Since Jesus himself was baptised by John, at the start of his ministry (e.g. Matt 3:13-17), the tradition did not have much of a head start on Christianity itself. Yet a small community has already been established at Ephesus in this tradition, at about the same time as a fledgling church is being founded.

In fact, these empires, with their concept of world domination, a common language, and relatively safe, efficient travel, created an environment in which the church could grow. And grow it did. There was a church in Rome itself while the Apostles were still alive (Rom 1:7) and, after about three centuries, Christianity became the state religion under Constantine.

Whatever you make of Constantine, the story moves on apace from there. While there are many books on church history, Patrick Johnstone, has done an exceptional job to bring the story up to date with his systematic surveys of the church around the world, conducted over the past 30 years and published periodically as *Operation World*. Another of his efforts in 1998, *The Church is BIGGER than you think*, shows just how impressively Daniel's vision is being fulfilled. The summary below relies heavily on these sources.

Following the record that we have in Acts there have been a series of major expansions from AD 100 to AD 2000. For instance, the early church expanded around the Mediterranean, reaching as far as India, until about 450 AD. Next, the Celtic church reached western and central Europe over the next four and a half centuries – and so forth. The story is well worth exploring.

In 1792, William Carey published his estimates of religious populations around the world and discovered that about 18% of the world's population was Christian, in its broadest sense. Over the next 200 years, this rose to around 1 in 3 people on the planet. During the same period, the global population rose from around 730 million to 5.4 billion people – so the numerical growth has been amazing. In fact, the percentage of Christians fell back slightly during the twentieth century, with steep declines in Europe being nearly compensated for by robust growth in Africa, Latin America and Asia. Evangelicals are the fastest growing group on the scene, and if present trends continue, they are projected to represent almost one in ten people on earth by 2020.

Writing in England, where church attendance continues to decline, it is hard to grasp this world-wide dimension. A recent newspaper poll has reported that England is one of the most godless places on earth, so it is hard to grasp the vibrancy, growth and commitment that characterises the international scene.

And the church is a truly international feature today. Perhaps for the first time, it is also truly free of an empire – embedded, as it is, deeply in so many different cultures. Indeed, when we examine the penetration from the perspective of people groups, the way in which 'the huge mountain' has 'filled the whole earth' (Dan 2:35) is even more impressive.

Growing up in a missionary family, I was aware of some of the Christian developments going on around the world. I would hear, in the '80s, how the number of countries in the world was really a very poor guide as to how the church was doing, because it was quite possible to have many ethnic groups within a single country. Deprived of Scripture, or a church that worshipped in their own language, some cultures within a country might well have no option to explore the Christian message, even if it were widely practised by the majority community. Recently, we have become more aware of such cultural divisions. In some cases, ethnic cleansing and civil war has split states into two or more new countries.

Apparently the number of states and territories was up to 237 in 2001 but the number of ethno-linguistic people groups today is around 13,000! Here again, the last two hundred years has seen a massive change in the scene. By AD 1800, around 2,000 of these people groups had some experience of Christianity. By AD 2000 it is estimated that this number had reached almost 12,000.

Again, following the pattern of those early Jewish communities, there has been a massive initiative in translating Scripture into the languages of these groups. This time, instead of going global, Scripture has gone local, often involving the preliminary step of reducing the language to writing. Apparently, in AD 1800, you could have obtained the Scriptures in any one of 67 different languages. By 1900, the total was up to 537. By 2000, the estimate is that this had reached 2,800 languages. For the record, Zia Nodrat's contribution was to translate the New Testament into his own Afghan Dari dialect. This still leaves over half the world's 6,703 languages without the Scriptures in the vernacular, but the task of giving everyone the Scriptures in his or her own mother tongue is now within reach. Because of the distribution of language groups, many of those still waiting for a translation are actually very small populations – typically tens or hundreds of thousands of people.

Viewed from this perspective, Daniel's dreams sketch out a remarkable story that reaches to the present day. What did Daniel predict? 'In the time of those kings, the God of heaven will set up a kingdom that will never be destroyed, nor will it be left to another people' (Dan 2:44). Looking back, we can see that something began to happen from around Daniel's time until Jesus came and founded the church. From then on, it has grown to fill the earth. Although it has faltered and failed abjectly at times, it has permeated kingdoms and societies around the world. I find it a compelling story and commend it to you.

The beasts and the kingdom

I was discussing the material for this chapter with a friend of mine who helped me with something I wanted to cover. One of the keenest contrasts in the book lies between the beasts on the one hand, and the Ancient of Days and his followers, on the other.

If we consider the beasts, for instance, in Daniel's first vision, the beasts in sequence are wild, boastful, increasingly vicious, terrifying and violent (Dan 7:4-7). The one like a son of man (Dan 7:13), who replaces them, 'was given authority, glory and sovereign power; all peoples, nations and men of every language worshipped him. His… kingdom is one that will never be destroyed' (Dan 7:14).

At the heart of the visions, therefore, are two very different types of kingdom: one characterised by the boastful beasts who enjoy a brief spell of awesome power over huge empires, and the other which will fill the earth and last forever.

Church and state

Let's find a topical way in. The Bishop of Hulme recently questioned the hymn, *I vow to thee, my country*, on the *Today Programme*. The challenge is whether a Christian can endorse the patriotic love it expresses. I have always found it a slightly strange hymn and wonder whether it has been promoted in school assemblies as much by music teachers interested to make the connection with Holst, as for any theological content. However, the second verse of Sir Cecil Spring-Rice's hymn touches very directly on the tension between these competing kingdoms, as it focuses on 'another country':

We may not count her armies, we may not see her King;
    Her fortress is a faithful heart, her pride is suffering;
And soul by soul and silently her shining bounds increase,
    And her ways are ways of gentleness and all her paths are
    peace.

Whatever Sir Cecil's theology, he seems to be pretty clear that there are two types of empire and that the rules of one's own country do not apply to this other kingdom. As you read Daniel, the kingdoms of the beasts are not simply replaced by just another kingdom, something in the same mould but with a different face. The kingdom that supersedes them is a different type of kingdom.

Nowhere is this tension more apparent than when Jesus comes to describe his kingdom. It makes his parables of the kingdom both obvious and elusive. It makes his teaching hard to pin down. How in the world will the meek inherit the earth (Psa 37:11; Matt 5:5)? Why does he tell Pilate, 'My kingdom is not of this world. If it were, my servants would fight to prevent my arrest by the Jews. But now my kingdom is from another place' (John 18:36)? My take is that when he said that, he meant just that. When John returns to this theme in Revelation, the symbols of the two types of kingdom could not contrast more strongly – the Lamb and the beast (e.g. Rev 13:8; 14:1).

It seems to me that this is a message church leaders have been quick to forget in their pursuit of temporal power and influence. Constantine may have been the first to try and unite the exercise of political power with the business of Christian worship, but he was not the last. Calvin held a view in which the church would be fairly influential on the state, too. Nyall Ferguson, through his book, *Empire*, and the associated television series, has noted the impact of British evangelicals in the nineteenth century on the world around. More recently, the Moral Majority in the US sought to bring its perspective to the political scene. In the UK today, the Anglican Church retains a great deal of political leverage and the Archbishop of Canterbury is expected to comment upon many political decisions. Some of the results, such as the abolition of slavery, were clearly beneficial.

But for every win, there were plenty of losses. Ultimately, churches and empires have very different aims and different ways of achieving those ends. After all, politics is the art of the possible while faith asks us to practise the impossible. Politics involves consensus and compromise. Clearly, once you have been given a divine revelation, the scope for compromise or even consensus may be limited.

So how is the church to make an impact? Many Christian communions would see the political pursuit of social justice as a key aim of the church. Returning to Daniel and his second dream, we have to remember that the Ancient of Days does not fight, nor dialogue with, the rulers who rise to prominence and then fade.

I appreciate that this is a controversial view and many inspiring Christians do not see it this way. For what it is worth, I believe that whenever the church has shared power with the state, it has made a poor fist of it. On the whole, the state seems to have a greater immunity to the reforming power of the church than the church has to the corrupting tendencies of power. My take is that the church has tended to best fulfil its mission to be salt and light when it has not had the power to make the rules, and that it has generally lost the plot when it has had that power.

It also seems to me that heavenly and earthly kingdoms have very different ways of changing the world. By and large, the political way of changing things is through the law. The Christian way of changing things is to change the individuals and see change brought about through the cumulative impact of lives lived differently. The change in individuals comes through conversion and the indwelling of the Holy Spirit. You cannot legislate for that – 'But the fruit of the Spirit is love, joy, peace, patience, kindness, goodness, faithfulness, gentleness and self-control. Against such things there is no law' (Gal 5:22, 23).

In turn, citizenship comes through different channels for earthly and heavenly kingdoms. Empires have rules and bureaucracies to count and monitor. Sir Cecil outlines a different growth mechanism in the hymn we have just quoted: 'soul by soul and silently.' It may not even be obvious to a third party whether such a change has taken place. God reserves the right to know who has and who has not taken that step. 'Nevertheless, God's solid foundation stands firm, sealed with this inscription: "The Lord knows those who are his," and, "Everyone who confesses the name of the Lord must turn away from wickedness."' (2 Tim 2:19). Conversion is not like getting a birth certificate, or a passport, although it is understandable that churches would dearly love to formalise it in just such a way.

One of the great lessons of the Old Testament is that you cannot create a set of rules that will bring people to God. Given that, what chance of success (or right to attempt it) has the church to legislate for those whose views and beliefs place them outside the church – possibly in strong opposition to it? And it seems to me that Daniel bears this out. It is not clear to me that either Nebuchadnezzar's decree (Dan 3:29) or Darius' decree (Dan 6:25-28) were effective in promoting the fulfilment of Daniel's visions, although they may have made life easier for Jews around their empire.

The great strength of this vision of a kingdom outside of empires is that no-one is excluded or put off because of what a given nation does. A Christian political kingdom on earth would necessarily cause problems for anyone from a different nation. Paul accuses the Jews of his day of creating just such an obstacle to others, 'As it is written: "God's name is blasphemed among the Gentiles because of you"' (Rom 2:24). The vision in Scripture is that the kingdom of heaven will draw its membership from every ethnic group on earth: 'After this I looked and there before me was a great multitude that no one could count, from every nation, tribe, people and language, standing before the throne and in front of the Lamb' (Rev 7:9).

This is a real paradox – a kingdom that permeates without power, a kingdom that has no earthly base yet spreads everywhere, the Lamb that overcomes the beast. Scripture has many such paradoxes, most centrally in the saviour who dies to defeat death itself.

So should Christians stay out of politics? Hardly. If anything, the stories of Daniel, Esther and Nehemiah provide strong encouragement for those with a deep faith to engage in the exercise of political power. It is just that I see no sense, or mandate from Daniel, in trying to assemble a Christian political agenda. I am not surprised when I discover Christians popping up under different party banners. And my guess is that when we look back, with perhaps a few high profile exceptions, the most effective will have been those who got quietly on with serving their constituents in the most conscientious and godly way they could.

This leaves lots of loose ends, especially about the role that the church, as a corporate organisation, should play in society. But that is another mystery for another day.

Pulling it all together...

In summary, then, we have looked briefly at four ways into the book. We have seen the way in which small scale events are juxtaposed with the global, and the way in which Daniel seems to pick out some of those events in a way that his contemporaries would almost certainly have failed to do.

We have taken this scale issue further and considered the future as a fractal. In many ways, the situations we face and the people who seem responsible for our futures are very similar to those Daniel faced at the highest level.

A third approach is simply to try and follow the story from 'the time of those kings' through to the present day, to trace out a surprising story of a kingdom in power nowhere around the globe and yet in evidence almost everywhere.

Finally, we have looked at some of the paradoxes and contrasts between the kingdoms of the beasts and the worldwide kingdom ushered in by Jesus.

I hope there is something there that works for you.

Thinking it through

1. To what extent have modern states or empires set themselves up against God? How have they done this and how has it worked out for them?

2. Try to find two examples of the history-as-a-fractal approach to Daniel that would have helped you in your own life.

3. Compare Hab 2:14 with Luke 18:8. Does Scripture envisage that the church will be ubiquitous and dominant or almost extinct by the time Jesus returns?

4. Can the two options described in the previous question be unified in any way?

5. How do other faiths handle the religion/politics issue?

6. What are the strongest arguments in favour of the church formally engaging in political change? What evidence from the past 200 years might bear out or undermine these arguments?

7. You have been given the task of preparing a talk on Daniel chapters 10 and 11 – how might you proceed?

8. 'Church history is interesting but not terribly relevant.' Discuss.

9. 'But when the time had fully come, God sent his Son' (Gal 4:4). List 5 things that had happened between Daniel's time and the coming of Jesus that made it just the right time.

10. Identify and discuss three international events of the 20th Century in which Daniel's viewpoint would have differed from that of most Western Christians who lived through them.

11. In what ways was the coming of the Jesus a political event? To what extent did Jesus' birth transcend politics?

12. What is the most difficult political period that you have lived through? What has been your personal experience of God's protection over that period?

7

In the end of all time

Ultimately, the message of Daniel is not about an organisation permeating society around the globe. In Revelation, John gets a peek into heaven, and we have already discovered what he saw. 'After this I looked and there before me was a great multitude that no one could count, from every nation, tribe, people and language, standing before the throne and in front of the Lamb' (Rev 7:9).

The link event from global movement to heavenly worship is Jesus' second coming: At his trial, Jesus was questioned over and over about who he was and what he was about. 'Again the high priest asked him, "Are you the Christ, the Son of the Blessed One?" "I am," said Jesus. "And you will see the Son of Man sitting at the right hand of the Mighty One and coming on the clouds of heaven."' (Mark 14:61,62). Compare this with Daniel 7:13: 'In my vision at night I looked, and there before me was one like a son of man, coming with the clouds of heaven. He approached the Ancient of Days and was led into his presence.' This is the end game for Daniel.

An element of this is the grand finale, the fulfilment of a plan begun on earth. For Daniel, however, it also carries a note of judgement that settles the issues unresolved on earth. It is the Ancient of Days, for instance, for whom the court sits, before whom the books are opened, and who pronounces judgement in favour of the saints (Dan 7:21, 22).

So how are we to view this today? As a teenager and into my early twenties, I remember church teaching fixated on calculating the schedule of Jesus' return in rigorous detail, despite Jesus' assertion that, 'No one knows about that day or hour, not even the angels in heaven, nor the Son, but only the Father' (Matt 24:36). Unfortunately for many of these theories, the political shape of the world has changed radically since then and the predicted engagements between the superpowers look much less likely now.

Despite all the confidence and predictions, reality has not

obliged. I guess one result has been for the interest of Christians to drift away from eschatology and onto other things. It would be nicer had their attention shifted from the details and timetable and refocused on the inevitability of the event. I am sure Daniel has something important to offer eschatologists about the events leading up to Jesus' second coming. But given the amount of debate and division over what that something is, is it not reasonable to focus on the more obvious, if mundane, messages?

Peter's approach is quite helpful in this respect. He had heard Jesus' parables, which had been full of people who nipped off and took ages to return. The chief servant assumes that the delay indicates that the master is unlikely to return and starts to beat up the other servants. However, the master will return and settle accounts (Luke 12:42-46). The virgins wait so long for the bridegroom to arrive that their lamps run out (Matt 25:1-13). However, the bridegroom arrives and they miss out on the reception because they are searching for more oil. Despite the master-is-away scenarios (e.g. Matt 25:14-30), by the time Peter writes his second letter, the early Christians are starting to worry about the delay. The sceptics are not slow to make their point.

Peter's response is to move the accent from the timing to the inevitability of the event. 'But do not forget this one thing, dear friends: With the Lord a day is like a thousand years, and a thousand years are like a day. The Lord is not slow in keeping his promise, as some understand slowness. He is patient with you, not wanting anyone to perish, but everyone to come to repentance. But the day of the Lord will come like a thief. The heavens will disappear with a roar; the elements will be destroyed by fire, and the earth and everything in it will be laid bare' (2 Pet 3:8-10).

So where does that leave us today? I guess it leaves us with a mix of feelings and responsibilities. The main difficulty with a faith based on revelation, is that your scope for manoeuvre is often quite limited. While I believe the church has a responsibility in every generation to sit down and reconsider what the truth revealed to it really means, and while some of that new thinking can represent a significant development, there are some truths that are pretty basic. I cannot see that there is much scope for reassessing Jesus' amazing assertions.

Supernatural end, supernatural beginning

To try and set some context, it is worth looking at the other end of time, where our understanding of creation has undergone significant development, not just following the impact of Charles Darwin, but also with developments across a range of scientific disciplines. The spectrum of Christian belief aligns at one end uncritically with a full-blown evolutionary approach, through to a six-day creationist view at the other. However, even within such a range of viewpoints Christians still differ from society at large in accepting the central thesis of Genesis that there is a God behind the cosmological unfolding. The assertion that we are not an accident actually defines a chasm between Christian and secular communities, and this was the key element picked up by the New Testament writers. 'By faith we understand that the universe was formed at God's command, so that what is seen was not made out of what was visible' (Heb 11:3).

Even at the start of the church, the apostles were prepared to pitch this message to those with very different world views. 'The God who made the world and everything in it is the Lord of heaven and earth and does not live in temples built by hands. And he is not served by human hands, as if he needed anything, because he himself gives all men life and breath and everything else. From one man he made every nation of men, that they should inhabit the whole earth; and he determined the times set for them and the exact places where they should live. God did this so that men would seek him and perhaps reach out for him and find him, though he is not far from each one of us. "For in him we live and move and have our being." As some of your own poets have said, "We are his offspring"' (Acts 17:24-28).

From my own perspective, I think putting Genesis together with a current understanding of origins is not easy and there are places where I have to throw my hands up and admit that I just do not have a good solution. Certainly, there are resonances today between the creation story in Genesis and the current view of creation that were absent several decades ago. The scientific grasp of how stupendously unlikely it was that a big bang should throw up a balance of matter capable of sustaining a universe at all, and that it could lead to a life-supporting planet such as our own – all this hints at meaning beyond chance. The silence of the spheres is not deafening, but it indicates that we might live in a lonelier neighbourhood than we expected, and after decades of probing for life out there, the prospect that we are unique is still high on the agenda. It isn't evidence but it resonates with the scriptural view that there is something absurdly special about humanity:

> When I consider your heavens,
>   the work of your fingers,
> the moon and the stars,
>   which you have set in place,
> what is man that you are mindful of him,
>   the son of man that you care for him?
>
>   (Psa 8:3,4)

The idea of a creation event in the big bang and the current progress towards a theory of everything, adds a profound back-drop to those first creative words, 'Let there be light' (Gen 1:3). I guess you will want me to come off the fence and indicate where I stand. To me, the formulaic repetition in Genesis speaks of a highly structured description.

What does a highly structured description look like today? I think it looks like the tube map, or perhaps as it used to look before the philistines decided to cram more information onto the page than the concept would bear. Those straight lines, crisp curves and brightly coloured tracks speak of genius rather than ignorance about the exact position of stations around London. Because of this, the tube map gives the right answer to the ques-tions it was designed to answer but often provides the wrong answer to questions it was not designed to answer. If you ask questions about the order of stations along the lines or the places at which you can change from one line to another, you get the right answer. If you want details about the exact location of the stations, you need to find a different map.

Bill Bryson (*Notes from a Small Island*) is a fan of the map but has his usual humorous take on the geographical difficulties that it creates. He suggests you take a friend to Bank and arrange to meet at Mansion House. The map will, of course, enable your friend to make the journey, but after the changes and stops, they will have arrived just of a couple of hundred feet from where they set out. That the two stations are nearly in the same place is not evident from the map.

It shows how difficult it can be to provide a clear description that answers everybody's questions, but this approach has the unfortunate effect of raising a new set of questions around what is or is not a sensible question as far as Genesis is concerned. Nevertheless, I find the idea very helpful that the Genesis account is a supremely elegant, rather than a savagely ignorant, account. It has been accessible to generations and still means something in our generation.

And I have listened to some beautiful unfoldings that link a current view of the development of life to the Genesis account. Personally, I think the scene is still changing and I watch with interest. The contribution of linguists and DNA experts to the developmental debate is providing, as far as I can see, some useful new perspectives. I think that this is helpful and would expect there to be some surprises ahead in unifying all the evidence around a common understanding. As that develops, I believe the most helpful thing Christians can do is to note the resonances between the secular and scriptural viewpoints.

Given the difficulties in looking back, it seems that we need to be careful in looking forward, since the difficulties over creation are, if anything, much less than those encountered when we come to the end of all time. The secular prediction about the physical end to earth in the distant future, scorched perhaps, by a dying sun is not a great worry to most of us – we do not expect to be around when it happens. Even that description has a resonance of Peter's elements being destroyed by fire (2 Pet 3:10)! We have the odd scare that something cold and fast moving may whack us from outer space in the next few millennia, but our main perceived risk lies in making the planet uninhabitable ourselves. For much of the past 50 years the fear was that this might come about through nuclear war. Today, we are more worried about our own impact on the environment.

Against this is the scriptural picture of an intervention by the man who came and died in Palestine under a Roman administration two thousand years ago. Nor is it easy to see this as an essentially private consummation for true believers. 'For as lightning that comes from the east is visible even in the west, so will be the coming of the Son of Man' (Matt 24:27). Passages such as this make is very hard to strip the cosmic significance of the scriptural story away from some sort of earthly core. Whereas the creator's hand is often gloved throughout history, the scriptural prediction is that the gloves will come off in the end of time.

To me, Scripture paints a compelling analysis of the human condition and a solution to it, through faith in Jesus. To our essentially materialistic society, it carries the unappealing baggage of supernatural origins and endings and a bright miraculous thread that cannot be pulled from the fabric without wrecking the weave. The whole thrust, as a story of God's engagement with the humanity that he created, of repeated attempts to engage successfully, and of his incarnation as a man two thousand years ago, I find compelling. On that basis, I can embrace a prediction so staggering that I cannot understand it.

I cannot see that we are free to break this piece of teaching off and ditch it just because it will make us unpopular with our peers. In fact, in our generation of all generations, Daniel's vision of a worldwide movement most coincides with Jesus' own teaching about his return: 'And this gospel of the kingdom will be preached in the whole world as a testimony to all nations, and then the end will come' (Matt 24:14).

At least we are used to living our lives in the light of predictions that we cannot verify ourselves, except by waiting to see. The paper forecasts rain this afternoon, and so I am sitting in a café writing this while the rest of the family, with Granny and Papa, are walking around Blists Hill. Later, we plan to go to an inside attraction – Enginuity. Had there been no weather forecast, we would have done things the other way around and spent the afternoon outdoors. However, given the forecast of rain later in the day, we have plumped for an indoor attraction this afternoon. I've been tapping away for a couple of hours, now and the sun is as bright as ever. I will take a lot of flak if the rain fails to come, because there were good reasons to come here later in the day. But you pick your forecast and live by it.

What sort of people should we be?

Peter's contention is that we should live lives that would not be embarrassed, should Jesus return now. 'So then, dear friends, since you are looking forward to this, make every effort to be found spotless, blameless and at peace with him' (2 Pet 3:14). In an age where we find our time and affections drawn after so many activities, priorities and possessions, the teaching that this world is not the end should have a strong impact on the quality of our lives.

That is hard. The new car is tangible, Jesus' return is not – at least, not yet. The holiday abroad has a flight time and date, the second coming does not. The bigger house may impress our friends, our belief in Jesus' return will almost certainly not.

And yet the call of Daniel, and of Scripture as a whole is for those who believe in a God of the whole world to live differently. During times when the church has been under enormous pressure – and they may come again – this teaching would have been highly attractive to hard-pressed Christians. But my guess is that it is about as difficult to live by now as it ever has been. And that is the calling. Live in the expectation that the light of eternity might break through at any time.

Finally, this teaching adds an edge to the gospel as a whole. I heartily wish that there were no talk of heaven and hell in Scripture. I wish there were no return in judgement. I wish the world were just the most amazing bowl of cherries for everyone. Scripture tells me that God wishes it were that way, too. But it isn't like that. Scripture teaches me that there is a God who could think of no solution to the world's difficulties better than to give his only son to die for it. It tells me that he offers freely but not forever. So it matters what you believe – not just for now, but for later. Paul recognises that if Christianity is just to make us nicer people now, we are completely deluded – 'If only for this life we have hope in Christ, we are to be pitied more than all men' (1 Cor 15:19).

And so, Daniel's vision of this mountain filling the earth really matters. His view that the Ancient of Days will finally sit in judgement and settle everything justly matters, too. According to Daniel, people have a real choice to make. One of the great things about our society is that everyone knows we have a choice of faith. Even where people stick within the framework of faith that they are born into, they are confronted everywhere with the fact that they have options. People in the UK have been delivered from the apathetic norm that used to exist in which you trusted your vicar or priest to sort things out when you were born and when you died – and where what you did in between was largely up to you.

And our responsibility with this message is to present the option to people, clearly and credibly, backed by lives that look, on inspection, as though we really believed it. As far as I can see, the thing God most values about humans is their ability to make choices. Even in Daniel's experience, God is remarkably reluctant to force a person's will. That is why we have a responsibility to live credibly. That is why our message with the choice it extends is important. That is why Christians are pressing the spread of this message to the ends of the earth – often at enormous personal cost. That is why friends of mine – and perhaps friends of yours, too – have sacrificed large swathes of their lives translating the Scriptures into languages spoken only, perhaps, by a few thousand people. Because there is a real choice to be made. And everyone deserves enough information to make the choice.

I had hoped to finish this chapter by noting that the rain had arrived. As you might expect, however, it was not the timing but the inevitability of the rain that really mattered. Perhaps you have already guessed. The weather forecast was right and we were right to heed it. We stayed dry inside at Enginuity, as it tipped it down outside.

Thinking it through

1. What aspects of our culture make a cataclysmic finale easy to believe in and which ones make it difficult?

2. What aspects of a final, fair assessment appeal to people today, and which do not?

3. How was Jesus' return taught in the time of your parents and grandparents? How could it be best taught today? What elements will have changed with each generation and which elements are non-negotiable?

4. To what extent do you think that Daniel's reaction to the visions (e.g. Dan 7:15; 8:27; 10:16) is because of their colossal impact?

5. How can Christians best promote a perspective based on Scripture while fully respecting those whose religious or secular views are profoundly different?

6. If Daniel were around today, what aspects of our culture might he recognise immediately, and which might cause him the biggest surprises?

7. If Jesus had returned this afternoon, what things would you have wished to have been doing differently? What things might you have been proud to be found doing?

8. How should the behaviour of people who believe that Jesus is coming again, differ from the behaviour of those who do not?

9. Is producing a written version of Scripture in the mother tongue of every person on earth a good use of resources? What do you think it cost to translate the Septuagint? How much has recent translation work cost?

10. To what extent has the technology of our generation helped to take the message to every person on earth?

Prayer

We never discover how Daniel first learnt to pray. Presumably it was a skill that he took from Jerusalem to Babylon. Was this the greatest, perhaps the only, legacy that his father or mother left to him? There is a hint at some sort of prayer life in his resolve before God not to take the king's food and drink (Dan 1:8). His reliance on prayer soon becomes explicit when he urges his friends to plead with God and when he responds later in gratitude after Nebuchadnezzar's dream and interpretation have been revealed to him (Dan 2:18-23).

It is because his enemies discover him 'praying and asking God for help' (Dan 6:11) that he is thrown into Darius' den of lions. In fact, the whole plot, with its peculiar demand that, for a month, all prayer should be directed solely to the king, was hatched just to catch Daniel out. And then, towards the end of his very long life, his career takes a new turn as an intercessor before God for his nation. We have already seen how Daniel's career seems to develop away from the secular and into the spiritual, with specific turning points, first with the visions, and then with this departure into prayer for the nation.

Daniel's prayer in chapter 9 ranks beside a few others in Scripture – Abraham's haggling with God (Gen 18:22-33); David's prayer of gratitude to God over the succession (1 Chron 17:16-27); Solomon's prayer of dedication for the temple (2 Chron 6) and Jesus' own prayer for the church (John 17).

As we have noted, this is not a totally new element in Daniel's life. He has cultivated a life of prayer, consistently, intently, under pressure and over decades. And for Daniel, there is a specific event that spurs him into action. He has been reading Jeremiah (Dan 9:2) and he realises that the duration of the exile is reaching the seventy years that Jeremiah predicted. There are a couple of passages in Jeremiah that he might have been studying – chapters 25:7-14 and 29:10-14. The first passage describes the exile as a punishment for the monotonous years spent provoking God in idolatry, hotly pursuing other gods. The second passage has a completely different tone – presenting plans and a bright future beyond the exile.

The latter passage is probably much more familiar to us. Jeremiah 29:11 has been discovered by many who face uncertainty or whose path ahead has been obscured. Out of the balance of these two very different takes on the same event, Daniel is drawn to cast and offer up one of the most remarkable prayers in Scripture.

Why pray?

In chapter 29, Jeremiah has written to the exiles. He encourages them to settle down in their new surroundings, to get their heads down and seek the welfare of the host nation. At the time, Jeremiah's message had seemed treacherous and subversive. The more patriotic prophets were predicting God's spectacular intervention. Hananiah (Jer 28:1-17) has appealed to the long tradition of backing your words with striking drama, so when Jeremiah wore a yoke to symbolise the journey into exile, Hananiah took it and broke it, with a bold proclamation that Nebuchadnezzar's power over the nations would also be broken within two years. If we take our time cue from Jeremiah 28:1, then long before the people have a chance to judge Hananiah's two-year prediction, the prophet of bright futures is dead (Jer 28:17) and Jeremiah urges the exiled Jews to settle in for the long haul. While Daniel may have recalled some of the heat of that early argument, the intervening years must have built confidence in Jeremiah's prophecy. So why bother to pray?

There seem to be two very different schools in prayer – those who pray for things because they believe they are unlikely to happen otherwise, and those who pray for things because they believe God has decided to do them anyway. I guess the first school is the more easily understood. My children take that tack with me. They do not plead to be taken to school (even though, for the most part, school is good fun). They do not generally plead to go to beavers, cubs or scouts. Meals, too, come and go regularly, and although a growing son seems to consume about 15,000 calories a day, the boys do not deem it worth their while to urge every meal onto the table.

Where there is more of a risk, however, there is more of a concerted campaign. Christmas lists are assembled with great care, lest parents unfamiliar with the current toy scene should squander the opportunity. A couple of years ago, we had a list compiled from the Argos catalogue, complete with prices and ordering information. This year, we found a rather bulky envelope in October addressed to Santa in our youngest son's bedroom. Before that, there had been a lot of cutting up of catalogue pages, just to make sure Santa got the details right. And I think a lot of our praying is like that. I wonder, in passing, whether the visualisation some Christians go in for is just a slightly more sophisticated attempt to point to the pictures and show God what we want.

Latent in our prayers, so often, is a belief that God may forget about us if we do not pray about it. Betjeman captures this self-centredness in prayer in his poem, *In Westminster Abbey*, especially the couplet asking protection over 189 Cadogan Square.

Jesus advises us not to get hung up on these things: 'So do not worry, saying, "What shall we eat?" or "What shall we drink?" or "What shall we wear?" For the pagans run after all these things, and your heavenly Father knows that you need them' (Matt 6:31,32). And yet Jesus encourages his followers to ask their heavenly father for the things they need in everyday life: 'Ask and you will receive, and your joy will be complete' (John 16:24). Clearly, asking for things is not wrong – although the accent lies on what we need, rather than what we think God is likely to forget to provide.

The opposite school emphasises waiting upon God and praying along with what is already planned. If we pray in accordance with God's will, our prayers will be fruitful. Couched in those terms, of course, it would be impossible to disagree. In its extreme form, this involves praying where there is no risk. If it is going to happen anyway, why pray?

So what sort of a prayer person is Daniel – is he into high risk praying or no risk praying? Does he pray because he is sure the exiles are bound for Judea, or because he sees a serious risk that they are not? As you will have guessed by now, I'm not sure that cutting the problem in this way is helpful.

Back to basics

My guess is that to gain some insight into Daniel's praying, we need a better concept of what he thought the exile was all about.

My hunch is that he was praying out of the situation, rather than praying against it, or praying for what he wanted to happen next. Clearly he gains part of his understanding of the exile from having lived in Babylon for the best part of a lifetime. When he first made the journey, a life as long as his may have seemed unlikely. Perhaps he is surprised and encouraged at the way things had worked out since – at least as far as he is concerned. However, it is unlikely that he would have missed some of the downside experienced by his fellow Jews. Psalm 137, for instance, explores the sadness, the jeers, the insane cruelty and utter hopelessness of exile. Alongside these mixed experiences, there will also have been a theological understanding.

The Jews in the Old Testament had a thing about the land. From Abraham's time onwards, the land was God's gift to them. 'The Lord had said to Abram, "Leave your country, your people and your father's household and go to the land I will show you"... So Abram left, as the Lord had told him; and Lot went with him... Abram travelled through the land as far as the site of the great tree of Moreh at Shechem. At that time the Canaanites were in the land. The Lord appeared to Abram and said, "To your offspring I will give this land." So he built an altar there to the Lord, who had appeared to him' (Gen 12:1...4...6, 7).

However, the promise came with strings and the small print is laid out graphically in Deuteronomy 28. If the nation obeyed and honoured God, they would be blessed in the land. Having dealt with the upside, the contract turns to the terms and conditions that would apply if the nation forsook God. Towards the end of this list, there is the following: 'The LORD will drive you and the king you set over you to a nation unknown to you or your fathers. There you will worship other gods, gods of wood and stone. You will become a thing of horror and an object of scorn and ridicule to all the nations where the LORD will drive you' (Deut 28:36, 37).

To build this understanding into the national psyche, the Israelites were expected, periodically, to split into two teams, climb a pair of opposing mountains (Gerizim and Ebal) and belt out the blessings and curses to one another across the intervening valley (Deut 27:12,13). A ceremony along these lines is reported in Joshua's time (Josh 8:30-35).

As we move on through the Old Testament, it is not surprising to discover that Solomon is most insightful. He includes the risk of deportation in his dedicatory prayer for the new temple. 'When they sin against you – for there is no one who does not sin – and you become angry with them and give them over to the enemy, who takes them captive to a land far away or near; and if they have a change of heart in the land where they are held captive, and repent and plead with you in the land of their captivity and say, "We have sinned, we have done wrong and acted wickedly"; and if they turn back to you with all their heart and soul in the land of their captivity where they were taken, and pray toward the land you gave their fathers, toward the city you have chosen and toward the temple I have built for your Name; then from heaven, your dwelling place, hear their prayer and their pleas, and uphold their cause. And forgive your people, who have sinned against you' (2 Chron 6:36-39). Interestingly, God's response does not offer an automatic way back to the land (2 Chron 7:12-22), notwithstanding the familiar passage that begins, 'If my people…'

Although many of the threats outlined in the original agreement materialised over the years and the Israelites became familiar with oppression and invasion, the risk of actually losing the land appeared minimal for hundreds of years. The book of Judges has a repeated pattern in which the Israelites cycle through disloyalty, invasion, repentance, and deliverance. But deportation? Losing the land? Impossible!

Until the exile, no one had had to sit down and work out the implications of losing the land. Now that they have messed it up so badly as a nation that God has dragged them, apparently, well over the brink and into disaster – how should they respond? For the first time in the nation's history, someone has to think it through. So where do you turn when you have to work something like this out? From the text, we know that Daniel has been thinking through Moses' message (Dan 9:11) as well as Jeremiah's.

Praying out of situations

Whatever our theology of prayer, for most of us, prayer is a tactical affair. Most of our prayers tend to take Captain Kirk's approach: 'Beam me up!' Desperation prayers, like every other type of prayer, have their place for the exiles. Remember Nehemiah's dilemma when the king grants him his wish? 'Then

I prayed to the God of heaven, and I answered the king' (Neh 2:4b,5a).

However, Daniel reminds us that God expects more of us – particularly after a lifetime of prayer. It is hardly surprising that the strategic visionary should have something strategic to offer us in prayer. My guess is that most of our prayers (certainly most of my prayers) lack much perspective. When we pray, we tend to see exactly what everyone else sees. There is a war: we pray for peace. We pray against aggressors and for the underdog. There is a famine: give now, pray for later. There is a crisis of government, we pray according to our politics. No time to think, just pray!

To take this forward, we need to return to a theme we explored in trying to understand the visions – namely the way in which Daniel sees things in a way that others do not. Sometimes it is easier to see the problem from a distance. I have already mentioned Nyall Ferguson's TV series, Empire, which I caught sight of one evening a few months ago. I noted the stress he laid on the nineteenth-century evangelicals. In one sense it was heartening, since the TV treatments of the eighteenth and nineteenth centuries in the UK tend to ignore the religious revivals and even the industrial revolution to forage for more politically correct content. On the other hand, I found the linkage he made between the empire and the spread of Christianity disturbing.

Coming from a missionary background (albeit nonconformist and interdenominational), I did not recognise the cosy relationship he had spotted between church and empire. My parents had quickly dropped out of the social whirl that circulated around the embassy, although they maintained a number of friendships within the expatriate community. Having said that, I did benefit as a child from one link with the embassy in the mid-sixties, when a PA found time out to come and tutor me. Her name was Jacqueline and I can still remember her writing 'b' on one hand and 'd' on the other to help me tell them apart. I also remember we did a sum once with very long numbers, because she wanted me to learn that the length of the numbers did not make the maths any more difficult. And then, me and the empire, we split – presumably when Jacqueline was posted elsewhere.

Again, coming from a tradition where missionaries within

living memory had left for the field, sometimes to die in short order, I found it surprising that Ferguson did not correlate their sacrifice with the ultimate harvest. I had known Jesus' analysis from childhood: 'I tell you the truth, unless a grain of wheat falls to the ground and dies, it remains only a single seed. But if it dies, it produces many seeds' (John 12:24). Even now, I am not at all clear how it works, but it attuned my outlook to detect such coincidences.

Given a more missionary-friendly perspective on revival movements, too, I was surprised that he linked the current widespread practice of Christianity across Africa so closely with Hyram Maxim and his gun. I have just finished Stephen Lungu's, *Out of the Black Shadows*, and have appreciated in a new way how effective national leadership was identified, trained and generally built up. It also highlighted the subsequent impact of that leadership over the last quarter of the twentieth century.

Still, I was intrigued by Ferguson's treatment and put his book, *Empire*, on my birthday list (back to lists of presents!). I greatly enjoyed the narrative and am following up with Brian Stanley's, *The Bible and the Flag*. I had gained a third perspective on a piece of the empire-and-church puzzle through *Way to Glory*, John Pollock's biography of General Havelock. Havelock was a professional soldier who became a Christian and was credited with relieving Lucknow, following the Indian mutiny.

The Indian mutiny is an example of evangelical influence cited by Ferguson. I am not an historian, but the story goes that the mutiny was triggered by the introduction of animal by-products into the cartridge casing that had to be bitten off before they could be fired. This was anathema to vegetarian Hindus. In the subsequent uprising, a great deal of violence was directed at the European population and when word reached England, the country (churches included) was up in arms. Something had to be done about this. Ferguson quotes Spurgeon, no less, making some highly inadvisable statements from the pulpit.

In the end, the uprising was quelled. Havelock was dispatched to relieve Lucknow and attention at home drifted, in time, to other things. But how had the evangelicals gone wrong? As we have already seen in attempting to interpret the visions, there is a problem if we only see what others see. In this case, they were affronted, along with everyone else at home, at this attack on the empire. But what business had they to be affront-ed? We may be asking too much in expecting those Christians to stand back and see the bigger picture before they preached their sermons. We all find it intensely difficult to stand back from our culture and see what is really going on. And yet that is exactly what Daniel calls us to do.

Daniel can see that the situation out of which he is praying has centuries of history behind it and the potential for unutter-able glories to come. While recognising national blame, he can see beyond national self-interest and he prays in confidence that God has a game plan that stretches out in all directions and embraces a string of empires ahead.

So how can we stand back and pray strategically? It seems to me that there are a couple of clues. The first is to get some his-tory under our belts. It need not be written-down history – although it will be tricky to master this perspective without any reading. It may involve talking to the elderly in our church to discover how God worked half a century ago. It may involve films or videos. It may simply involve familiarising ourselves with the pattern of God's hand at work throughout Scripture.

A second clue may come from the media. I don't know whether you remember the story of the Enigma machine that coded German messages during World War II and required such ingenuity and good fortune to crack. The beauty of the design was that a letter could be encrypted into almost any let-ter – and that it would not necessarily be the same letter the next time around. I say, 'almost' because the only thing for certain was that a letter would never be encrypted as itself. This seemed like a very small clue, but you knew that an 'e' in the encryption, would never turn out to be an 'e' in the plain text. It seems to me that the same probably applies to our media, with its short-ter-mism and secular analysis. My take is that it is a safe rule of thumb specifically to rule out those things that are agitating the media, in seeking for strategic direction. After all, there will be a different set of exciting worries for tomorrow.

That is not to say we should take no interest in current affairs. Far from it! I would just suggest that whatever analysis is being pressed upon us may be safely left aside for the purposes of strategic praying. A surge in the price of petrol, Tim Henman making it to the semi-finals in Paris – these were hot topics yes-terday, but are unlikely to fuel strategic prayer. Having said that,

I very much enjoyed watching Tim win!

What about the new Iraqi government, announced yesterday? Should we be praying about that? Certainly. But the agenda Paul sets out on government is quite different from the current analysis. 'I urge, then, first of all, that requests, prayers, intercession and thanksgiving be made for everyone – for kings and all those in authority, that we may live peaceful and quiet lives in all godliness and holiness. This is good, and pleases God our Saviour, who wants all men to be saved and to come to a knowledge of the truth' (1 Tim 2:1-4). There is certainly an agenda for prayer – one that we can pray on behalf of Christians on the ground in Iraq: that they may enjoy open and peaceable government that recognises freedom of worship and allows them to share their faith with their friends.

But it seems that we are called away from the two main lines of current analysis. On the one hand, it is for the politicians to decide whether this will prove a decisive step in the war against terror. On the other hand, the voters must decide what they make of the war (and currently they seem to have swung against it). It is not that these perspectives are unimportant but rather that, as Christians, there is a different set of priorities. We, too, have a big game with everything to pray for.

A promise for dark days

Perhaps this was the passage from the Pentateuch that had grabbed Daniel's attention as he meditated on his people's plight in the light of Jeremiah's prophecy: 'When all these blessings and curses I have set before you come upon you and you take them to heart wherever the Lord your God disperses you among the nations, and when you and your children return to the Lord your God and obey him with all your heart and with all your soul according to everything I command you today, then the Lord your God will restore your fortunes and have compassion on you and gather you again from all the nations where he scattered you. Even if you have been banished to the most distant land under the heavens, from there the Lord your God will gather you and bring you back. He will bring you to the land that belonged to your fathers, and you will take possession of it. He will make you more prosperous and numerous than your fathers. The Lord your God will circumcise your hearts and the hearts of your descendants, so that you may love him with all your heart and with all your soul, and live' (Deut 30:1-6).

Some years ago, I worked on Daniel for a series at church. The talk on prayer, however, fell during the visit of an outside speaker, so he took it. Because I had put in some effort and had gotten interested in Daniel's prayer, I wanted to do something on this passage myself. A month or two later, I was speaking at another church and decided to dust off Daniel's prayer as a stand-alone talk.

One thing became clear to me as I worked on it. I realised how insignificant the promise in Deuteronomy of rescue from a distant land must have seemed before the exile. What comfort is there in a promise of rescue if you never think you will need it? How dull and perfunctory this promise must have seemed – of course it would be okay in the end. My guess is that the promise took on a new sparkle from the depths of the exile, when the Jews realised what a spectacular promise they had in God's commitment not to forget them. After the horror of exile there was hope in the promise: a way back, even from here!

That there is always a way back is one of the great teachings of Scripture. As I read it, there is only one sin that cannot be forgiven, and that is against the Holy Spirit (e.g. Matt 12:31). Like many, I used to worry a great deal about this sin, and wonder whether I had committed it. If we consider the context in which Jesus first spoke about it, as well as the balance of Scripture, it seems to me that such a sin must be one for which repentance is impossible, and therefore one which no Christian would commit.

Apart from that, the incredible truth is that God offers forgiveness fully and freely to anyone who asks. Indeed that is the very introduction Jesus uses in discussing the unforgivable sin: 'And so I tell you, every sin and blasphemy will be forgiven men' (Matt 12:31). For those who want to explore these ideas a little further there is a question at the end.

Disasters we make for ourselves

But I believe there is another important message here, namely, that when we have really messed up, when we feel that no-one would ever want to have anything to do with us again, God is still there, offering forgiveness and a way forward. I tried to bring out in the talk that some promises only shine in the darkest circumstances – and the message was brought home, rather tragically, to me that day.

Although I had not expected it, a friend of mine who had been a church leader elsewhere, was in the congregation. He had recently been in court, had pleaded guilty and was awaiting sentencing. Shortly afterwards he went to jail. Alongside my own struggle to come to terms with this news, I realised that my friend had a lengthy and difficult journey ahead. It would be the same sort of trek that David had had to make following his affair with Bathsheba and the murder of her husband, starting with admission, repentance and restoration (2 Sam 11:1-12:25). His psalm captures the point well:

> Do not cast me from your presence or take your Holy Spirit from me.
>
> Restore to me the joy of your salvation
> and grant me a willing spirit, to sustain me.
>
> Then I will teach transgressors your ways, and sinners will turn back to you.
>
> (Psa 51:11-13)

Daniel's prayer, then, is alive with the realisation that there is always a way back. We appreciate how radical this is when we present the gospel message to those who have not had a conversion experience. But do we believe it for those who mess up after becoming Christians? Most people believe that Christianity is basically for good people. In fact, the offer of salvation is made exclusively to bad people. We are only eligible if we recognise our own sinfulness. 'On hearing this, Jesus said, "It is not the healthy who need a doctor, but the sick. But go and learn what this means: 'I desire mercy, not sacrifice.' For I have not come to call the righteous, but sinners"' (Matt 9:12,13).

The theology here is twofold. On the one hand, God declares those who trust in Jesus righteous, an argument that Paul works out in some detail in Romans 4. On the other, the Holy Spirit takes up residence and begins to turn the proposition into reality (see, for instance, Rom 5:1-5). In a sense the first step is an act of pretending on God's part. God pretends that we are holy because he intends to make us so one day – 'But we know that when he appears, we shall be like him, for we shall see him as he is' (1 John 3:2b). Too often, however, we forget that we are very much work-in-progress. Too often we start pretending that we are better people than we are, and indeed, the charge of hypocrisy is one of the most frequently levelled accusations against Christians today.

So can we recognise that Christians are capable of great falls and that for them, too, there is a way back? So often we think – I think, if I'm honest – that Christianity is a second chance but that if we mess up again we are on our own. Daniel's insight is that God's people are never alone, even when their predicament is largely one of their own making. Wherever we are and however we got there, Daniel reminds us that we can always turn to God in prayer. And from that perspective, the promises of forgiveness and restoration shine more brightly than ever.

The role of repentance

In a sense Daniel's understanding of the road to restoration for the nation lies along the same route that David had to take – acknowledgement and repentance, before making a return. But what if the nation has not learned the lesson? What if there has been no repentance? What if there has been no acknowledgement that the national behaviour has outraged the God who gave them the land? Has the nation learned the lesson? As he looks around the nation, he probably sees many things to discourage him. Nonetheless, Daniel is driven to pray. Furthermore, it seems that his concern has developed over a period of time (see Dan 9:3), which hints that the prayer that has been recorded for us was part of a much longer process.

So how do we know if repentance has taken place? If it is someone else, does it matter to me? Surely, unless someone has specifically sought my help in such a matter, it is none of my business how far he or she has made it along the road to restoration. Although it sounds kindest, there may well be times in which this laissez faire approach turns out to be quite cruel, because it may prevent us from fully trusting that person, or entrusting them with responsibilities, again. The Prodigal's father, for instance, recognises his younger son's repentance at the deepest level and so is prepared to lavish his resources upon him once more, even though he has squandered a fortune (Luke 15:22-24). While the father's love is much tougher than his son's rebellion, he also knows, from his son's abject confession (Luke

15:21), that the young man has learned his lesson. He can be trusted in a way that he could not be trusted before. He really has found a son who was lost to him before (Luke 15:32).

There is a minor example of this in the case of Mark, who deserted Paul and Barnabas on their first adventure (Acts 15:38). A question mark remains over Mark, which unsettles the team so much that Paul and Barnabas eventually split (Acts 15:39). The rift between Paul and Mark heals eventually, and Paul comes to trust Mark once more (2 Tim 4:11). More seriously, with misdemeanours that involve an element of habit, it may be important to establish the degree of repentance.

Certainly, a spell of punishment will not necessarily guarantee repentance. A friend of mine lives in a house called Repentance Cottage. Apparently, it was once a reform school, and a pair of dormitories was knocked together, and with the associated complex, forms the present house. The local pub was called *The Drill* and, having a rural setting, the sign painter had assumed the name to refer to a seed drill. It was more likely that the drill was square bashing, intended to punish the unfortunates who were sent there.

Misconceptions, of course, are not confined to sign painters near old reformatories. Punishment and repentance do not always go together, however harsh or humane we try to make the system. A recent television programme explored the attitudes of some lifers in British jails. I missed the programme, but read the TV critic the following day. She explained how she had approached the programme with a liberal view and had emerged quite angry. She had expected contrition, with evidence of concern for the victims' families. Instead, she reported on inmates who were all too ready to complain about the treatment they had received from the system. Well, are the Israelites contrite or whinging?

Daniel feels constrained to lay down a marker. Someone has to admit that the Israelites have been wrong. Somewhere it has to be recorded that God was just and the Jews were wrong. Someone needs to take some responsibility in ensuring that the link between the original punishment and the ultimate restoration foreseen by Jeremiah is properly bridged by acknowledgement and repentance. In an amazing piece of advocacy, Daniel comes to realise that he can be that someone. Four times he repeats the refrain, 'We have sinned' (Dan 9:5,8,11 and 15). It is possible that he does not speak for all the deported Jews, but he manages to speak for those who eventually return, chastened, dependent upon God and determined to do things differently.

Forgive them their trespasses

I am surprised, as I read the prayer, that Daniel seems to confess so many sins that it seems unlikely that he ever committed himself. From what we know, he had not turned away from God's commands or laws (Dan 9:5), nor had he ignored the prophets (Dan 9:6). We have just noted how it was a prayerful consideration of the work left behind by two of those prophets that led him to pray in the first place. So how do we reconcile his confession with what we know of the man?

First, it is likely that Daniel is aware of some personal guilt before a holy God. The more Daniel discovers of God and his standards, the more acutely he is likely to be conscious of his own shortcomings. For instance, when he says, 'We do not make requests of you because we are righteous, but because of your great mercy' (Dan 9:18), surely he is speaking honestly on his own behalf as well as on the part of others. You have probably noticed this: many people who have drawn very close to God have a deep sense of their own frailty and failures. We see this reflected in the incarnation. Moses says, 'You shall not commit adultery' (Ex 20:14). Jesus says, 'But I tell you that anyone who looks at a woman lustfully has already committed adultery with her in his heart' (Matt 5:28). The closer you get, the more probing the standard.

Before we move on to look at the way in which Daniel sees himself as a representative of the exiles, there may be a further reason why he feels he can confess sins and failings that he may not have done. The phrase, 'There, but for the grace of God…' springs to mind. I used to think it a rather condescending thing to say, an aloof mix of relief and arrogance with a nod to the doctrine of original sin. However, the older I get the more I realise how true it is. I remember reading somewhere that there was nothing to stop crime like comfortable surroundings, a good upbringing… and witnesses. How many turning points can we look back on, where a slightly different set of circumstances might have led us down very different pathways.

I once heard a story (Elizabethan times? Georgian times?)

about someone who sent a letter to a dozen noblemen with the message, 'Fly at once, all is discovered!' I understand that most of them were out of the country in a trice. The letter was a weird sort of joke, but the impact was all too scary. I wonder what would happen in our churches if someone were to circulate a similar message. But even where there is nothing to hide, most of us are aware of how close a call it was. Agur, son of Jakeh, has it right:

Two things I ask of you, O LORD; do not refuse me before I die:

Keep falsehood and lies far from me; give me neither poverty nor riches, but give me only my daily bread.

Otherwise, I may have too much and disown you and say, 'Who is the LORD?'

Or I may become poor and steal, and so dishonour the name of my God.

(Prov 30:7-9)

Perhaps Daniel sees God's hand in his life, steering him away from a nationalism that would have proved his undoing and preserving him from a critical spirit by providing for his needs. As he has retained his position of influence, he has plenty of evidence of what might have happened had he put a foot wrong. Maybe he remembers friends and colleagues, deported with him and with whom he shared so many aspirations, fears and views. Maybe they just seemed to drift ever so slightly apart at first, and now Daniel looks back over very different lives. Maybe Daniel recognises how easily it could have been the other way around.

The 'we' word.

But even after we have identified all of these possibilities, after we have pushed Daniel's confessions to the personal limit, the passage makes no sense unless we also recognise that Daniel is praying on behalf of others – probably others who are unlikely to start praying for themselves. This is vicarious praying. Daniel is acting as an advocate, a barrister even. He is representing other people, and he does so where they most need his support. So why is Daniel able to do this?

The answer that springs immediately to mind is that Daniel appeals, as an Israelite, back to the promises that God first made to Abraham and confirms through Moses. As a Jew, he is able to appeal on behalf of the nation that has received special promises. As a leader, Moses was willing to argue the nation's case before God (e.g. Exod 32:9-14). But why would Daniel feel led to step up to this? Perhaps, because of his high birth, he feels a sense of responsibility for the nation as a whole.

My guess is that, like Isaiah and others, he sees something needs to be done, and then it dawns upon him that there is no one else willing to take on the task – 'Then I heard the voice of the Lord saying, "Whom shall I send? And who will go for us?" And I said, "Here am I"' (Isa 6:8).

And sometimes it is as simple as that. You have a burden to see something done. You are sure there are much better qualified people than yourself but somehow they have other things to take up their time. There is a rather cheesy joke about a bloke who worried about what happened to the sun every night. It worried him so much that eventually he decided to stay up all night and find out what was going on. And the next morning it dawned on him.

And so often, while we may never really understand why, it dawns on us that this one is our call. And it does not take a sense of the superiority of others to make us shrink back. There may be all kinds of reasons why we think others should step forward. Perhaps we have a lot on our plate already. Certainly, if you are in leadership, a healthy habit is to try and offload as many tasks and responsibilities as possible. Those that refuse to go away may well be your special task. And these exilic Jews seem aware of this sense of unexpected calling in a new way. Remember Esther?

Esther is quite happy to be special and live in the palace, but there is also a sense in which she shrinks from tackling the king about the decree to eliminate the Jews. The king loves her – why should he discover that she is a member of a despised minority? Mordecai will not let her get away with this (Esth 4:14): 'And who knows but that you have come to royal position for such a time as this?'

However it is, then, Daniel not only recognises the need, but realises that he is the man for the task. And so, 'I prayed to the LORD my God and confessed: "O Lord, the great and awesome God… we have sinned and done wrong"' (Dan 9:4…5).

A friend who reviewed this chapter reminded me that there is a current scenario in which you take responsibility for actions you may not have committed yourself. Board members of a company share a common responsibility for individual decisions. Until recently, this responsibility was taken quite lightly, and to be a non-executive director was a cushy number – a nice salary at minimal risk for a relatively light workload. However, following some high profile corporate governance cases, the roles of all directors are coming under fresh scrutiny. You may go to jail for what the finance director gets up to – so keep yourself informed!

Are we as Christians today in the same position to pray in this way for the nations in which we live? Of course? Well I am not talking about praying for those around us as, 'they' – they have sinned and done wrong. Somehow, 'they' must turn into 'we'.

Back in the '70s, especially around the time of the Festival of Light, I remember that people liked to quote from God's response to Solomon's prayer of dedication, after he had opened his new temple; 'If my people, who are called by my name, will humble themselves and pray and seek my face and turn from their wicked ways, then will I hear from heaven and will forgive their sin and will heal their land' (2 Chron 7:14). The deal seemed to be that if Christians in the UK prayed and humbled themselves, God would look with favour on the UK. You may notice that this analysis would create an earthly kingdom of God a bit like other kingdoms. As we discussed in trying to interpret the visions, we are looking for a heavenly kingdom that is different from other kingdoms, and so this diagnosis presents difficulties anyway.

But even as a teenager, I felt there were other things that were wrong with this analysis. It seemed to me that the whole thrust of salvation was that people are forgiven personally for sins that they confess personally. How can I confess someone else's sin? Furthermore, it seemed to me that the national treaty that God made with the Jews in the Old Testament had no national parallel in the New Testament. The whole legal basis on which Solomon could appeal, and on which God could reply, was missing as far as we were concerned in the UK in the '70s.

My conclusion was that we could not pray that kind of vicarious prayer for our friends, neighbours, and fellow-countrymen. A new deal had been struck through Jesus, based on personal faith, and the prayer game had moved on. Which is a bit of a relief, really, since the blame Daniel accepts on behalf of his fellows is severe. So we can treat this part of Scripture as a purely historical account without ever having to apply it to our lives. Nice. Easy. Move on.

Hold on! While the underpinning agreement between God and our nation may not exist in the same way for us today as it did for Daniel back then, and while we may not feel that ethnic bond that knit Jewish society together in a way that modern cosmopolitan societies cannot really appreciate, we do have a very strong basis on which to join Daniel in praying for the people in our nation. We are just like them.

I cannot remember what I was reading that first pointed me to this analysis, but it was very helpful to me. Those who love and worship God through Jesus may not have done all the things that those around have done, but they are driven by the same appetites and aspirations. Too often, the lack of wrongdoing is not down to a lack of intent, but to the presence of restraint. In a very real way, we can be completely honest in joining in Daniel's prayer and listing all our failings. The failings of those around us are our failings, too.

The heart of God

Through Daniel's efforts to pray for his fellow Jews, we find out more about the heart of God. There is a response from heaven. Almost everything about the response is perplexing – maybe it all meant more to Daniel than it does to us. But let us not worry too much about that. Daniel prays, an angel encourages him and, in time, the Jews are free to return home. The return does not feature directly in Daniel's record. My take is that the return itself does not matter. The tension is gone and everything is going to be okay. The timing of the actual return is immaterial now – it is no longer a case of whether but when.

Is intercession for me?

My guess is that intercession is a ministry that takes time to develop. The blend of insight and awareness needed to be effective may take most of a lifetime to acquire. Daniel's example (and there may be counter examples in Scripture) is also that it is a time-consuming role that may cut in as other calls on our time recede. Perhaps it is an early example of the sort of inner growth Paul talked about that runs counter to the natural decay that goes with aging. 'Therefore we do not lose heart. Though outwardly we are wasting away, yet inwardly we are being renewed day by day. For our light and momentary troubles are achieving for us an eternal glory that far outweighs them all. So we fix our eyes not on what is seen, but on what is unseen. For what is seen is temporary, but what is unseen is eternal' (2 Cor 4:16-18).

Is this for you? Do you sense the same concerns that drove Daniel to prayer? Are other things happening in your life that may indicate a new ministry is opening up? Has your training and career left you with a broad vision and strategic view of life? If so, maybe Daniel is an exemplar for you. Maybe his intercessory style is a good one for you to follow.

And what if it looks like intercession isn't for you? After all, we are called to engage at some level even in ministries that are not our specialty, so to speak. For instance, we are all called to generosity (e.g. 2 Cor 9:7), but there will also be those with a special gift in giving (e.g. Rom 12:8). In other words, even if giving is not your special gift as a Christian, you are still expected to be a good steward with the resources God lays at your disposal and to be mindful of the needs of others, generously if possible.

And with this in mind, Daniel reminds us of our general responsibility to pray for our friends and neighbours as well as distant nations. He furnishes us with an agenda as to how we should pray and provides us with some ideas on informing ourselves. As I write, I am once more aware of how poorly I perform in this area. For a while, with my older two sons, we used *You Too Can Change the World* by Daphne Spragatt as a way of praying for the world (it is a sort of junior version of Patrick Johnstone's *Operation World*). However, writing this up reminds me of my need to find something systematic to support my personal prayer life for the world.

How can I make this work for me?

I struggle with this, because I am so conscious that my own prayer life is not anything like it should be. For most of us, prayer is a difficult duty that we avoid if we can. If we are honest, we find it lacks relevance and excitement – and it frequently takes an emergency to draw us into anything like meaningful prayer. If so, take heart! It is the emergencies in Daniel's life – particularly his working life – that fuel his early excitement in prayer. My reading is that some personal interaction before God would have been part of his dietary resolution (Dan 1:8-16), but it is overtly there when he returns to his friends and urges them to, 'plead for mercy from the God of heaven concerning this mystery' (Dan 2:18) so that he will be able to interpret the king's dream.

So let's thank God for the trials we face, the times when we are at our wits end. We all pray better when we are in trouble – and I sure that God knows that. That our everyday lives, our working lives, our unremarkable lives, should throw up so many opportunities to pray in desperation is a blessing. It may not seem a very holy way to pray. Better we feel, to start from a position of disinterested neutrality. Then we could really pray. But God knows us much better than we know ourselves. Look at the Psalms! How many of them are clearly set in times of distress and personal danger? It is certainly the case for me – the times I have experienced the deepest prayer life have been those in my life that were characterised by least security – a job change or a car that is packing in. Prayers of this sort help us to overcome one of the barriers to prayer – our lethargy. When we are pumped full of adrenaline feeling that we must do something, and yet know can do nothing else, we can turn to prayer. And there is a reward in that.

Brief payers, focused and to the point, are a great place to start, but they often have another benefit – once the crisis is resolved we have something to say thank-you for. It is interesting that, while we do not know exactly what Daniel's friends prayed before he received the revelation of the king's dream and its interpretation, we have a lengthy passage of poetry that Daniel wrote to commemorate the escape and to offer something back to God by way of thanks (Dan 2:20-23). We are not very good at saying thank-you in our society and may even be suspicious of notes of thanks or congratulations – what are these people really after, we ask ourselves? It does not look like things were any better in Jesus' day – remember how only one man returned to say thank-you out of the ten who were healed (Luke 17:11-19)?

A brief thank-you? How about writing a structured prayer, or even a poem, as Daniel does? The nature and length of Daniel's paean of praise suggests a degree of experience with this form of praying. It suggests, to me anyway, that saying thank you by composing his own response of praise to God, was something he had done before – perhaps many times before. Practice, repetition… perfection.

At first sight, this type of structured response might seem a little over the top, a bit too keen. In our culture, the writing of songs and the composition of formal prayers are traditionally left to the experts – but not in all cultures. Breaking out with this type of response seems to come naturally to educated men such as Daniel and Zechariah (Luke 1:68-79), but also to the less educated Hannah (1 Sam 2:1-10), Mary (Luke 1:46-55), or even the Apostles who string snatches of psalms into their prayer (Acts 4:24-30).

Starting with a psalm can be a helpful way into this type of composition. I find that the trick with meditation is to find a way to slow everything down so that you can actually engage with the themes. Trying to recast it in your own words, or to restyle it as an expression of your own experience, gives you that time.

And I have tried it. For what it is worth, here is something I worked on, based around Psalm 84. The psalm has some wonderful imagery – of birds in the building, of pilgrimage and protection – and it has that haunting sense of longing. There are also difficult snatches – for instance, those pools that spring up in the Valley of Baca. But, if your family can put up with you for a few days while you puzzle it all out and start to sculpt some words and phrases for yourself – here is what you might end up with:

> There is a place of praise and rest
> Beyond our best and wildest dreams,
> Where even sparrows find a nest
> And swallows flit between the beams.
> And all the worshipers below
> Are lost in longing for your face,
> Enjoying, as their praises flow,
> The beauty of your dwelling-place.

Now pilgrim souls have heard a drum
That sets their pulses running fast.
In ones and twos we see them come,
Converging to a stream at last.
For man and woman, girl and boy,
A high protector rules the sky
And rivers flood the land with joy
Wherever they are passing by.

O Lord, Almighty, hear my prayer,
For even years of bright resorts
Would fade beside a session there -
A day of worship in your courts.
Instead of all I've done before
Or all that I could hope to do,
I'd rather stand and hold the door
And let another pilgrim through.

The God of Jacob is a sun,
A shield for every pilgrim band.
He saves the best for everyone
Who seeks protection at his hand.
O, give us all the words to say!
Increase our longing for your face!
And as we worship here today,
Accept us in your dwelling-place.

If you want to sing it, Vikki Cook's modern tune to *Before the Throne of God Above* works well and was the template I used. Whatever your approach, taking time with the psalms, or composing your own psalm from scratch, as Daniel has done, may help you and sustain you in your prayer life.

In conclusion…

So, let's not be ashamed if our prayer life begins in what we would regard as rather selfish territory. The combination of prayers uttered in desperation and the thanksgiving afterwards provides a robust and motivating way to begin. Let's not be afraid, either, of trying things that we may have to stick at for a while, in order to fashion prayers and songs that express our thanks to God.

As we get into praying, Daniel encourages us to look at problems in a different way. His approach to analysing what the real problem is, and in deciding how to pray about it, will fuel the content of our prayers. Choosing to see things differently, to watch for different things, and to avoid the knee-jerk reactions in prayer, are guidelines especially associated with Daniel and his strategic perspective on life.

We do not know how he progressed along this road, but by the time he is an old man, prayer is completely embedded in his lifestyle. It is such a distinctive and, indeed, widely known feature of his life, that the administrators and satraps are able to build a preposterous scenario around it and take their request to the king (Dan 6:6-9) – purely because they want to destroy Daniel.

So how do we get to that level of embedded practice? In terms of behavioural change, I was taught a simple model that has four stages. In the first stage, you are blissfully unaware of your shortcoming – unconscious non-compliance. You do not know, for instance, that you never say please or thank you. The next stage is perhaps the most depressing – conscious non-compliance – where you become aware of the problem and realise with exquisite embarrassment that you have just committed yet another faux pas. After that it is onward and upward – conscious compliance – where you can get it right if you think about it. This stage is hard work, but if you stick with it, you reach the final goal of unconscious compliance – you do it naturally, without even thinking. I suppose driving is a bit like that: you start out as a child, issuing hearty encouragements to the driver to overtake or go faster. Later, when you start learning to drive, you cannot imagine how anyone can think about everything that is going on inside the car and on the road. With practice, you get on top of things. You still struggle to remember to look in the mirror before indicating, but at last you iron these behaviours out. And then you can drive without really thinking about the details. You can concentrate on what the boy on the bike in his blue Chelsea strip is thinking or whether the girl yelling to her mates on the other side of the road is about to dash across to join them. And I think prayer is a bit like that – moving from unconscious failure to unconscious mastery.

Both learning to talk and learning to drive require a tremendous amount of effort, and usually we need to be highly motivated in order to invest the effort. In both of these examples, there is a significant pay-off and so we can appreciate where the motivation comes from. Perhaps that is why we need problems to stir us to prayer.

But Daniel's life has one more thing to teach us about prayer. We have noted Daniel's easy way with relationships on several occasions, and in particular the bedrock of his relationship with God. In the end, it is all relationship. In fact, relationship is all that God has to offer us, and prayer plays a central role in mediating that relationship. As any relationship deepens, it becomes more impenetrable to the outsider. My take is that one of the reasons that Daniel is a difficult book is that, eventually, his relationship with God has too much unspoken content for us to understand. They understood one another much better than we understand either.

The thing about relationships is that, while it takes rules and practices to establish a relationship, eventually, the rules recede or dissolve. And it is a bit like that with Daniel's praying in the end. At times it seems hard to differentiate what we would call reality from what we would call prayer.

One of the truly rewarding things about watching your children grow up is to see the way they use language. It starts with the imperatives – the need for a drink or to make it plain that they want this cereal instead of that. It starts with raw survival, but it does not end there. With teenagers wandering about the house, mobiles occasionally pressed to their ears, or messaging their friends in a text language that trips effortlessly from their fingertips, you can see that communication is as much about variety as content. They talk to make each other laugh, and sometimes to wind one another up. They make sage observations and silly jokes, create wild and surrealistic scenarios, and relate stories from their lives that have brought them joy or sadness. They talk about things that they cannot understand and about things that you cannot understand. They wander around reading funny cartoons out to everyone else. But through it all, they are building relationships – with their parents and with one another – and they are also building the capacity to build further relationships. And ultimately, you cannot legislate about that – which is, I think, what Paul had to say on the matter, too (Gal 5:22,23).

That is the end game for each of us. We may find that the relationship is mediated by profound utterance and punctuated by deep silence. We may find that it is mediated by bursts of chatter and song. Ultimately it is not about the form our praying takes, but where our prayer takes us in our relationship. Over to you.

Thinking it through

1. How did you learn to pray? Who or what has helped you to develop a life of prayer?

2. List three things that you think God has been doing in your life over the past five years. How will these factors help you to pray out of your present situation?

3. Who are the strategic prayer specialists in your fellowship? What have you done to encourage them in their ministry? What new ideas might you pursue, in the light of Daniel's experience?

4. A Christian friend asks for a chat and you discover, when you meet up, that she has been caught with her hand in the petty cash till at work and has been fired. What questions would you put to her and how would you counsel her in the short term and for the long term?

5. A chap in his twenties who has been converted for just over a year comes to you because he believes he has committed the unforgivable sin. You check for a history of mental illness and discover there is none. How would you proceed in advising him?

6. You have been asked to run a monthly prayer meeting. Bearing in mind how boring prayer meetings can be, how would you plan and prepare for the first three months?

7. What do you think are the top five global issues for prayer? What are the top five political issues? How do the two lists compare?

8. What area of your prayer life do you think needs most development now?

9. What is the greatest spiritual need of your five nearest neighbours? To what extent is this also your need?

10. List five major national moral failures. To what extent are these also serious issues within the church?

11. How far can we go in taking responsibility for the sins and shortcomings of other people in the church?

12. Cain asks the question, (Gen 4:9), 'Am I my brother's keeper?' Taking into account Jesus' teaching on our neighbours (Luke 10:29-37), how far does our moral responsibility for others extend? Where does this take our praying?

Globally local

There has never been a generation in which the local and the global have been so closely integrated. One of my sisters lives in Ethiopia. Her daughter has been suffering from an illness that has worsened over several weeks. By the end of last week she was advised to return home and has already had a consultation in the UK. There are few places on the planet more than 72 hours away from Heathrow. The reverse journey is also straightforward and you can get people almost anywhere – even during their annual holiday. Many churches have had the experience of sending teams of young people to participate in church projects in Africa or South America during the summer vacation. The daughter of some friends of ours is off to spend her university vacation in Christian service in Japan. I was in my late twenties before I made it as far afield as Japan. The world is just getting more and more accessible.

International news reaches us within hours. The war in Iraq affects the price we pay for fuel at the petrol station down the road. We have access to food, fabrics and even furniture from all over the world. Call centres in India ring me up a couple of times a month to sell me loans or insurance. If ever there was a generation that should take its global responsibilities seriously, we are that generation. Daniel wrote for us.

The good news is that there is a Christian vision for the world. It is not a new vision – it predates Christianity itself! The vision is not one of worldwide domination. In fact, Jesus paints a very pessimistic picture, in places (e.g. Luke 18:8): 'However, when the Son of Man comes, will he find faith on the earth?'

But the vision from Daniel, and amplified by Jesus, is one of worldwide presence and consequently one of worldwide choice. 'But you will receive power when the Holy Spirit comes on you; and you will be my witnesses in Jerusalem, and in all Judea and Samaria, and to the ends of the earth' (Acts 1:8). 'And this gospel of the kingdom will be preached in the whole world as a testimony to all nations, and then the end will come' (Matt 24:14).

As we have seen, there is much to be encouraged about in this vision. The growth of the church – rooted now in all sorts of cultures around the world, and the way in which Scripture has been translated into so many languages – is an astonishing story that has reached a new climax in our era. All this is greatly encouraging, especially to those of us living in England, where practising Christians seem fewer and farther between than they have been for decades, if not for centuries. Maybe Daniel appears to be stating the obvious to congregations across Africa and in both American continents.

But sometimes a global perspective is a frightening perspective. There are some powerful forces out there and some very scary people. Perhaps this helps to explain the evident discomfort that Daniel experiences through his visions (e.g. Dan 8:27; 10:2,3).

So how does the book end? In a flash of glory? Is there some arcane twist in the detail? No! The closing verses of Daniel become very personal. Whatever his past positions of influence, Daniel is still a small person in a big and dangerous world. And so the final passage is full of hope and reassurance, 'As for you, go your way till the end. You will rest, and then at the end of the days you will rise to receive your allotted inheritance' (Dan 12:13).

Whatever the grandeur and turbulence of the visions, the enduring image I am left with is of a humble man quietly getting on with life. He started as little more than a highly privileged slave, his whole existence hanging precariously in the balance. The trick was to realise that the balance was not held by the king, nor was it subject solely to winds of unpredictable change. Daniel learned that his God held the balance, for him as an individual and, indeed, for the empire. It does not turn out that way for everyone. Zia Nodrat, for instance, the blind Afghan I mentioned earlier, was persecuted and appears ultimately to have given his life for his faith. There are martyrs elsewhere in Scripture, but Daniel takes us back to the quiet, confident walk with God.

And that surely is where we need to finish – back to the basics of walking with God. In our working life, a call to work, to manage, to serve conscientiously and with compassion. At home, a call to create a secure and loving environment for those around us. In a sense, nothing has changed for Daniel – it is business as usual. It is not that the mysterious is about to be extinguished by the mundane. Rather, the majesty of his calling can only be complete in a well-lived, commonplace existence.

Getting on quietly with life is not something I am particularly good at. I like a bit of challenge and excitement. I have to say that I am not so good either with the uncertainty and stress that tend to accompany the exhilarating lifestyle. While there are prophets who call us into the wild and unexpected, it is important that we savour the moment with Daniel before we leave. It is going to be okay. God is still in control. Daniel's life has been a sustained and lengthy discovery of how in control God is and now, at the end of his days, there is the promise of peace and an inheritance. Let's leave Daniel, then, with a quotation from another prophet, Micah:

> And what does the LORD require of you?
>   To act justly and to love mercy
> and to walk humbly with your God.

(Mic 6:8)

Thinking it through

1. In what way will this encounter with Daniel change your priorities?

2. In what ways would you most like to be like Daniel? In what areas are you most different at present?

3. From now on, how will your life make a difference around the world?

4. How do you feel called to make more of an impact among the people who know you best?

5. You have been asked to take a Sunday school series for three weeks on Daniel. What themes would you like to take to 7-8 year-olds?

6. You have been asked to prepare a series of half-hour talks for the weekdays of an over-50s holiday. One of them has asked you to look at Daniel – which aspects of Daniel would you feel are most appropriate?

List of books referred to in this study

A colleague suggested the books alluded to needed to be formally listed somewhere, and so, for those interested in wider reading, here they are. Few were written with Daniel in mind, but looking at the list now, it provides a very interesting backdrop. I think Trevor Harris' *Moving God's Finger* is probably out of print, but I've tracked down a version of each of the rest – often through the Internet.

Frank Abagnale with Stan Redding *Catch me if you can*
Scott Adams *The Dilbert Future*
Jonathan Aitken *Pride and Perjury*
Jonathan Aitken *Porridge and Passion*
Joyce Baldwin *Daniel: An introduction and commentary*
John Betjeman (selected by John Guest) *The Best of Betjeman*
Corrie Ten Boom *The Hiding Place*
Bill Bryson *Notes from a Small Island*
G K Chesterton *The Everlasting Man*
Charles Colson *Loving God*
James Gleick *Chaos: Making a New Science*
Mark Greene *Thank God it's Monday*
Byron Farwell *BURTON*
Niall Ferguson *Empire: How Britain Made the Modern World*
Robin Lane Fox *Alexander the Great*
Patrick Johnstone *The Church is BIGGER than you think*
Patrick Johnstone and Jason Mandryk *Operation World*
Richard Layard *Happiness: Lessons from a New Science*
C S Lewis *Mere Christianity*
C S Lewis *Miracles*
Stephen Lungu with Anne Coombes *Out of the Black Shadows*
George Orwell *Animal Farm*
John Pollock *George Whitfield and the Great Awakening*
John Pollock *Way to Glory*
Simon Singh *Fermat's Last Theorem*
Brian Stanley *The Bible and the Flag*
Daphne Spraggett *You Too Can Change the World*

Partnership Guides

Practical help for local church groups and individuals.
Note: all titles 216 x 135mm

A Guide to God's Family
Being Part of Your Local Church
Stephen McQuoid

A practical introduction to life in a local church. Topics covered include God's view of his family, what the family gets up to, finding your niche, joys and responsibilities, family structures, and "the awkward squad". Brief chapters are supplemented by discussion questions, and suggestions for further reading.

978-0-900128-22-6 / 96pp

Sharing the Good News in C21
Evangelism in a Local Church Context
Stephen McQuoid

This book looks at the changes that are taking place in our society and asks the question, how do we reach that society with the Gospel? It starts with an analysis of the lessening impact of the church at the beginning of the twenty-first century, and then suggests how individual Christians can reverse this trend by involving themselves in the lives of unchurched people so as to win them to Christ.

978-0-900128-25-7 / 128pp

Stephen McQuoid is the Principal of Tilsley College, which is part of the ministry of Gospel Literature Outreach. He travels widely preaching in churches throughout Great Britain as well as lecturing in the College and writing. He and his wife Debbie are involved in a church planting work in Viewpark, Uddingston, Scotland.

Jake
Just Learn to Worship!
Terry Young

This book was written by an unemployed Church Elder as he waited to find out what would happen next. In the circumstances, Jacob was a great character to study and write about. Jacob lived a tough life, full of uncertainty, whether as a third-generation nomad, a farm hand for his uncle, or waiting for an uncomfortable reunion with his elder twin. Add to this a series of turbulent relationships plus a chaotic family life, and we have a picture that is very recognisable today.

978-0-900128-27-1 / 108pp

After the Fishermen
How Did Jesus Train his Disciples?
Terry Young

This book considers the approaches Jesus used to train his followers and then looks around to see how relevant they are today. From a non-specialist background more as trainee than trainer, the author finds that many of Jesus' methods are still around. However, while churches may be using them, it is probably secular management training organisations that are putting them to greater use.

For anyone who has been sent on an interviewing course, or has been taught how to run a meeting or conduct an appraisal, this book is a chance to explore ways of applying that training to Christian service. Most chapters conclude with a set of questions to explore the ideas further and to help in adapting the suggestions to one's own situation.

978-0-900128-28-8 / 102pp

Terry Young was born to missionary parents who eventually returned to the Midlands where he attended the local schools and university. In 1985 he moved to Essex for a job in industrial research. More recently he has become a Professor of Healthcare systems. In 1988 he married Danielle and they have served actively in their local church. They have three boys.